# The Lynmouth Flood Disaster

by

Tim Prosser

ISBN: 0 9541803 0 5
First published in Great Britain in 2001
Reprinted 2004, 2012
Lyndale PhotoGraphic Ltd.
Riverside Road, Lynmouth, Devon. EX35 6EX.
Telephone 01598 753778

# The Lynmouth Flood Disaster

by

Tim Prosser

# Contents

# Preface

Water is paramount to all life on our planet. Besides its obvious sustenance, when harnessed correctly it provides all manners of benefits to society. Industry, sanitation, creation of electricity, its uses for washing, cleaning in so many guises proves of infinitesimal value to us all. Water can be frozen, boiled, and vapourised, the list is endless with regard to the demands we ask of this truly invaluable and versatile compound.

Even our thoughts are stimulated by it. Vast oceans, calm lakes, busy streams and meandering rivers all play an essential part on our emotions with the variety of views that water offers us. Painters can be stimulated by it. Poets are inspired by its many moods.

Water is indeed good to us, but it can run out of control, it can wreak havoc, it can flood, and it can drown us.

Many lives were lost when the North Sea vented its awesome uncontrolled power on the East coast of Britain in January 1953. Only five months before on August 15th 1952, extreme rainfall over Exmoor lay waste an unsuspecting North Devon village that was beloved by so many. Twenty-eight lives and fifty five buildings were lost from the tiny resort of Lynmouth. In total, thirty-four lives and ninety-three buildings were claimed in the North Devon and West Somerset area that day.

There is no doubt that in one night the heart of Lynmouth was taken both structurally and communally. Consequently, the village was redesigned to a plan that would never allow the devastation caused to happen again, yet successfully retain the character of a unique and beautiful village.

Lynmouth does not and indeed has never laid claim to the artificial and contrived attractions that other resorts boast of. Instead, it offers the permanent, dramatic, and natural features of its various sea and landscapes to the discerning visitor.

This fact is confirmed as Lynton and Lynmouth is one of only three areas in Britain officially recognised as an area of "serene tranquillity".

## Lynmouth

By the middle of the 18th century, the upper class of British society was changing its attitude toward rural areas. Instead of treating the countryside as forlorn or even hostile, they felt an affinity with the countryside as they moved into the 'romantic' period of history.

When the French Revolution started in 1789 the gentry of Britain were dissuaded from crossing the English Channel to admire the grand landscapes that Europe offered them. Unable to journey abroad safely they turned their attention to the picturesque and dramatic scenery of their own country.

Lynmouth's reputation as a tourist resort started when these visitors found the open moors, steep narrow valleys and high sea cliffs a perfect substitute for the grandeur of the continental scenery denied them. The credibility of the resort was established when the poet Percy Bysshe Shelley honeymooned with his young bride Harriet Westbrook at Lynmouth in 1812. This unexpected interest in the village came at an opportune time for the residents. The herring which their livelihood had depended upon for centuries, had virtually disappeared from this area of the Bristol Channel by 1797. The people of Lynmouth had faced a bleak future.

*Lynmouth 1813*

Early tourists were particularly attracted to the East and West Lyn rivers that tumble over rocky beds down high steep wooded valleys to meet at the heart of the village.

The name Lyn is derived from the Saxon "Llynna", meaning torrent, which typifies the mood of both rivers after heavy rainfall on Exmoor has caused them to spate.

On very rare occasions, however, these two bubbling rivers that gave the village its name and added so much to its character, could flood to a point where the small resort and its residents were under threat.

The village had suffered a devastating flood from the Lyn rivers in 1769. According to *A History of the Parishes of Lynton and Countisbury*, by John Frederick Chanter, M.A. who was Rector of nearby Parracombe in 1907.

> "The river at Linmouth by the late rain rose to such a degree as was never known by the memory of any man now living, which brought down great rocks of several ton each. Large boulders were washed into the harbour and boats were smashed. Fishermen's cottages were left in a ruinous state".

Records of this flood are few, but it appears that it was comparable in ferocity to the 1952 flood.

Late 18th century prints of the village show few houses and no river walls to restrict the flow or block trees and debris brought down by a flood. If any flooding occurred, the water could dissipate easier. Another extreme flood in November 1859, resulted in four feet of water entering the Lyndale Hotel although village buildings suffered little structural damage.

*Lynmouth circa 1850*

The lower part of Lynmouth was built on the delta of the Lyn rivers as steep valley sides restricted building higher up the village; consequently most properties were sited close to the riverbanks. As the demand for buildings grew with an increasing tourist trade during the 19th century, level sites became scarce. In 1893 the wealthy publisher, George Newnes, settled in Lynton when he built his home, Hollerday House, on a hill overlooking the town. His great love of the twin resorts resulted in him financing schemes that were to encourage more visitors to the area in the late 19th century. Access between Lynmouth and Lynton, 500 feet above, was made easier with the building of the water powered cliff railway in 1890. A two-foot gauge railway running through the North Devon countryside was built in 1898 linking Lynton with the main line station at Barnstaple twenty miles away. Both projects were encouraged and financed by the great benefactor.

In 1894 George Newnes announced that a pier would be built at Lynmouth to cater for the many paddle steamers that plied the Bristol Channel. The promise of this increased trade led to the business community investing heavily in the resorts. The result being a demand for building sites within the limited flat areas that Lynmouth offered. With the flood of 1769 forgotten, hotels and shops were erected wherever there was space. The pier was never built; financial support by wealthy residents was withdrawn when they realised the villages would be overwhelmed with rowdy day-trippers. In 1895 when demand for property was at its height local businessman, William Bevan, built the imposing Lyn Valley Hotel at the mouth of the West Lyn river. On the opposite bank, the West Lyn and Granville Hotel were erected. Lack of space forced these buildings to innocently encroach onto the river where it joined the East Lyn; consequently, the narrow channel created was to have a devastating effect during the tragic flood 57 years later.

*The narrow West Lyn river*

*The backs of the buildings in Lynmouth Street*

## Coastal Erosion Theory

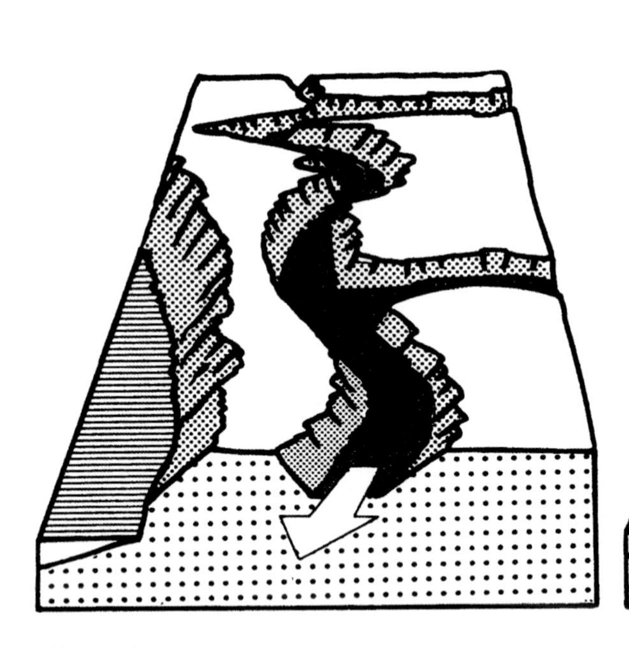

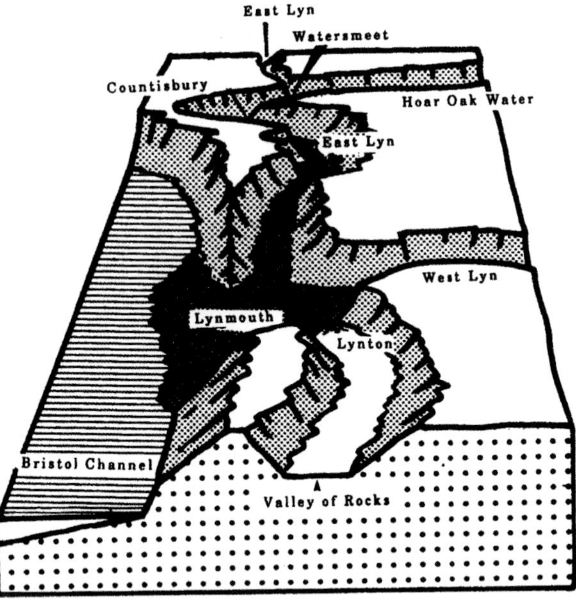


Stage A
The coast looking east as it might have appeared 125,000 years ago when the coastline was further north and the valleys were not as deep. It implies that at that time the Valley of Rocks was part of the Lyn Valley which had it's mouth further west.

Stage B
Subsequently the sea could have eroded cliffs until the side of the Lyn Valley was breached. As a result, the Lyn found a new way to the sea leaving its old lower course dry. The East and West Lyn cut gorges to the sea with renewed vigour.

## East & West Lyn Rivers

It is necessary to understand the character of the Lyn rivers as their geography is an important contributing factor to the nature of any flood they create.

The second smallest of Britain's National Parks, Exmoor, has its highest point at Dunkery Beacon set 1700 feet on the tableland of the moor. When walking across this high ground, what appears to be mile after mile of undulating grassland is deceptive. Suddenly, a narrow valley appears on this apparently uninterrupted landscape.

These numerous steep sided 'combes' that intersect the moor are where the headwaters of all Exmoor rivers start. Never far apart they leave little room for any flood storage. Those taking a

*The junction of the West (centre) and East (left) Lyn Valleys. Circa 1910*

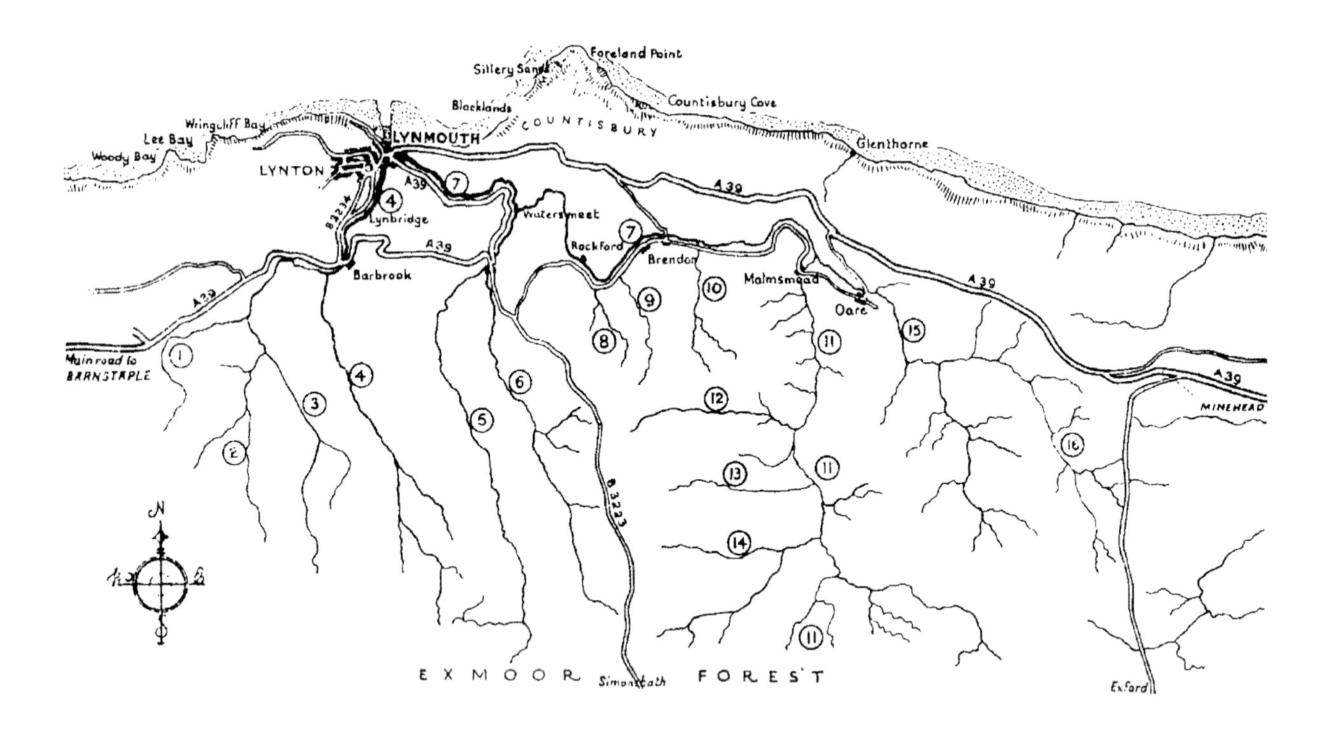


## Sketch of Tributaries of the East and West Lyn Rivers

1. Ranscombe Water
2. Woolhanger Water
3. Thornworthy Water
4. West Lyn River
5. Hoaroak Water
6. Farley Water
7. East Lyn River
8. Cranscombe Water
9. Tippacott Water
10. Coombe Lawn Water
11. Badgworthy Water
12. Lank Combe Water
13. Hoccombe Combe Water
14. Hoccombe Water
15. Oare Water
16. Weir Water

southerly route have a long journey to the English Channel and are of a gentler gradient than those taking the shorter route north to the Bristol Channel. The vast, intricate network of streams and tributaries of Lynmouth's rivers are illustrated by the map on page 6. Exmoor's high plain has above average rainfall of about 60 inches a year; compared to the lower slopes at Lynmouth for instance which collects an annual average of 40 inches. Never more than 4 feet thick, the soil of the high moor quickly saturates after heavy rainfall. This causes the headwaters to rapidly transform from a trickle into a fast flowing tumble over their stony beds.

The comparatively short distance that the north flowing waters travel from such a high elevation ensures swift movements of the rivers over their steep gradient from moor to sea. Unlike most rivers in Britain whose gradients reduce as they approach the sea, the character of the East and West Lyn rivers that meet at Lynmouth are opposite to the norm. Their gradients steepen as they travel towards the sea increasing the velocity of the water flow.

The East Lyn river rises about 3 miles from the coast to the west of Porlock village in Somerset. Initially flowing Northwest toward the sea as Weir Water, the high coastland hills guide the stream in a westerly direction where it runs unusually parallel to the coast for most of its twelve-mile length. Flowing through the fertile Oare valley, at Malmsmead it is joined by Badgworthy Water, pronounced 'Badgery', this is the river's largest tributary. The stream flows through the Doone Valley, the area of Exmoor made famous by R.D.Blackmore's historic novel, *Lorna Doone*. Along the Oare valley, the riverbed is at its gentlest with a gradient of 1:63, but once past the village of Brendon the East Lyn begins to get steeper. At Watersmeet, where Hoaroak Water joins the East Lyn, the river starts to drop dramatically. From this point the gradient increases to 1:27 until it reaches its journey's end at the Bristol Channel two miles away. The gradient of the East Lyn averages out at 1:50.

Geologically, it is only recently that the sea has captured the Lyn rivers. In the interglacial age, 125,000 years ago, the river ran less deeply entrenched (today, the Watersmeet valley is 200 metres deep). At that time, the river met the Bristol Channel eight miles further west near Combe Martin, the sea level being 100 feet higher than it is today. Sea cliff erosion, combined with the scouring action of the West Lyn joining the river at right angles created a weak point in the valley wall, which eventually breached. (See page 4).

The spectacular and powerful waterfall created by the release of the Lyn rivers into the sea would have created rapid downcutting of the river bed. Eventually the dried valley bed downstream of the breach was left progressively higher than the rivers. Today this isolated valley can be seen clearly 500 feet above Lynmouth. Sited at the eastern end by the small town of Lynton the valley opens out into the unique natural amphitheatre of the Valley of Rocks at the western end of Lynton. This valley shows the riverbed level at the time that the sea breached the Lyn rivers. The level of the river above Brendon can be accurately lined up with the floor of the Valley of Rocks four miles away. This line clearly indicates how much the East Lyn has cut itself back to Brendon since the river broke through to the sea. However, it is still in the process of regrading, leaving its tributaries hanging or discordant.

The gradient of the shorter West Lyn is much steeper than its sister river having an average fall of 1: 20. For the last 2000 feet of its course, this river travels as a series of spectacular waterfalls with a gradient of 1:5 through the Glen Lyn Gorge just before it meets the East Lyn at the heart of Lynmouth. This final steep section of the river was to have an extreme effect on the village during the flood.

*Lynton can be seen in its valley 500 feet above Lynmouth.*
*The West Lyn Valley is in the top left of this 1950 aerial picture.*

*The East Lyn Valley circa 1930. Tors Road is on the left of the valley and Watersmeet Road is on the right. The large building on the left of the picture is the Tors Hotel on Countisbury Hill.*

*West Lyn Cafe (left) and Lyn Valley Hotel (right) on the opposite banks of the West Lyn where it meets the East Lyn in the heart of Lynmouth.*

*Fishing from the backs of the buildings in Lynmouth Street Circa 1890.*

*A passenger steamer anchors off-shore bringing visitors to Lynmouth. Circa 1900*

*A popular view from the Lyndale Bridge shows West Lyn Cafe on the left. Circa 1930*

*PC Derek Harper on duty at Lyndale Cross shortly before the flood. The fruit shop and chapel that were later swept away are on the right.*

## The Flood

The first two weeks of August 1952 had been exceptionally wet. 6.5 inches (162 mm) of rain had fallen on the Exmoor area during this period. Visitors had cut short their holiday in Lynton and Lynmouth and returned home, some cancelled their bookings altogether.

The 15th August dawned with the promise of a little sunshine to break the spell of bad weather but by 10 am the sky had turned gloomy. By midday it was dark enough for lights to be switched on throughout Lynmouth. Heavy rain followed which continued incessantly all afternoon. An unnatural large black cloud tinged with red and purple hung ominously low and still over the village, making the people feel threatened and ill at ease. This strange cloud has been described as, "a huge pile of cumulus shaped like the beginning of an atom bomb explosion. Above the black base from which rain was falling heavily, cloud was swirling viscously. Yet above it the sky was clear and blue with only wisps of cirrus cloud." There was just cause for the feeling of foreboding amongst the 1700 people in Lynmouth that afternoon.

*The Lyndale Hotel circa 1900*

It was at about 3:30pm that the owner of the Lyndale Hotel, Tom Bevan, began to feel concerned. He looked outside and saw that rain was choking the road gutters and water was starting to pour into the hotel basement. Staff were mustered with mops and buckets but their efforts were all in vain. When beer barrels began to float around, the cellar was abandoned. The normally clear East Lyn river that ran alongside the hotel, was discoloured and was rising noticeably. Suddenly between 5:30pm and 6:30pm, the downpour was tremendous. Although the East Lyn was well above normal flood level by the time dinner was being served at 7pm in the Lyndale Hotel, it was still being held by its banks. When in spate the river was normally the colour of red Devon soil, an ominous sign was the black mass of peat that was now flowing towards the sea.

By 8 o'clock there was a rushing flow of water in the street 12 inches deep. Soon after, the hotel bar was awash with water up to the top of the 4-feet counter. The Lyndale Hotel was now marooned from the rest of the village.

As the raging torrent swept down the narrow valley gaining speed, it was joined by a multitude of overflowing streams that were now pouring from the steep valley sides. Large trees wrenched from the hillside joined massive boulders that were tumbling towards the village. To make matters worse, this debris jammed against the many bridges that crossed the river creating dams. As these blockages collapsed under pressure an overwhelming surge of water was released to vent even more of its fury on the little village.

*Lyndale Hotel (left), Granville Hotel (right).*

It was not long before disaster struck. A hundred yards in front of the Lyndale Hotel the West Lyn river suddenly swept the front of the Lyn Valley Hotel away. At the same time a wing of the West Lyn Cafe on the opposite bank crumbled into the river. The narrow channel innocently created by the erection of these buildings was beginning to have a terrible effect. The enormous boulders and trees being swept down the Glen Lyn Gorge soon blocked the narrow Prospect Bridge at the bottom of Lynmouth Hill. There was nowhere for the thundering water to go other than to flood over its banks and straight to the heart of the village. The mighty 30 feet high cascade that swept all before it enveloped the Glen Lyn Garage, Plymouth Brethren Chapel, a fruit shop and an adjoining house. Further down the village and directly in the path of this awesome flow lay the Lyndale Hotel.

Suddenly as the water was swirling against the hotel, four people were seen being swept against the wall outside. Basil and Barbara Eyers were hauled through the lounge window by willing helpers in the hotel. Luckily, the other couple were washed onto the saloon bar roof where they were rescued by dragging them through an office window. They turned out to be Beryl Pavey, the wife of local Police Constable Stan Pavey and her nephew from London, Michael Spry. All had been in the Eyers Fruit Shop when the diverted river overwhelmed the building.

A mass of water and debris suddenly poured into the Lyndale when the front door burst open. By now, everybody had hurried upstairs quickly saving what they could as they went. The noise was deafening as the West Lyn piled rocks and debris against the south wall of the hotel, which was now being attacked by both rivers. Still the sturdy building held its ground. As the level of boulders and debris built up to the first floor of the hotel, the water level was forced to rise both outside and inside the building. Now the forty-five frightened people had no alternative other than to seek shelter on the second floor as the threatening water level followed them upstairs.

*The water mark left by the flood can be seen below the top floor window on the Lyndale Hotel.*

It was at this time the main bedroom collapsed and fell into the flooded lounge. Shortly afterwards part of the opposite side of the hotel crashed into the East Lyn due to the constant onslaught from that river.

Alf Barson, an electrician from Leicester on a fishing holiday and staying at the Lyndale Hotel said "It was terrifying, as I was fishing earlier the water started to rise quickly. I dashed into the hotel and there must have been forty of us watching from the window downstairs. After a few minutes, the water rushed through the door and we all retreated upstairs, but still the water came up. We all went to the second floor but were only safe on the third floor. During the night we heard the floor below cave in as boulders broke through a window." He carried on saying, "The building was shuddering all night. We just sat there and talked, walking around sometimes - how we talked. We all got out at dawn through a broken bedroom window straight onto a pile of boulders."

By some miracle, the Lyndale Hotel protected its occupants until dawn by which time the waters had subsided. Firemen helped the survivors evacuate from a first floor window onto the boulders that had amassed against the hotel during the night. The only casualty was a budgerigar that had been swept away from the lounge with its cage. Later that day, a dirty watermark could be seen along the side of the hotel wall. It measured 55 feet (18 m) above the normal river level.

For Mr and Mrs Eyers, the traumatic experience had been too much. Besides their narrow escape from death, they had lost their fruit shop and home. Soon after the flood, they left the village to start a new life in Australia.

A widely held belief is that the Lynmouth Flood happened at night and was not witnessed by many people due partly to the loss of the Power Station blacking out the village at around 9 pm. It is true the main devastation occurred from mid evening onwards, and understandably no pictorial record exists of the actual happening. Photography is not uppermost in the mind when your survival is at stake. Television crews were not able to rush to areas of news as they do today, besides, video equipment was in the future as was satellite transmissions. Television was still in its infancy and very few people owned a set. Coincidentally, the BBC transmitter at Wenvoe in Wales bringing television to the North Devon area for the first time, started transmission on the day of the flood. Most people would visit the cinema weekly to see news events that had been filmed by Pathe or Movietone cameramen and these crews duly arrived the next day. Suffice it to say that the dramatic and harrowing record of film and photographs taken the next morning tell the story vividly enough. However, many people who were in the village at the time witnessed the scenes of destruction.

At about 6 pm, May Bridge, the footpath across the River Lyn to Rock House was awash and spilling water onto the Harbour road. Henry Pow, a young carpenter of the village, arrived early for the evening performance at the Pavilion. From his window seat in the Rising Sun at about 6:30 pm, he witnessed the increasing water level. He tells of “seeing the bridge gently rise, float away and then break up as the torrent carried it out to sea,” and of watching “large trees turning over in the water and reappear stripped of all branches and foliage”. The Tors Road footbridge higher up the East Lyn was seen to be lost in the same way a little earlier that evening by Fred Fouracre, who lived nearby in Summer Cottage, Watersmeet Road, with his wife Freda and baby daughter Lyn aged 2.

Fred’s mother called for them to come down to her house where she thought they would at least be a safer distance from the raging East Lyn. Fred and his family made their way down the flooded Watersmeet Road, in the blinding rain, to the shop and house of his parents. His father, ‘Ern’ Fouracre, was the manager of Medway’s butcher shop and Fred helped him in the business. On the family’s arrival they found Fred’s sister, Evelyn and her husband Archie Holsgrove there. Concern for his wife had led Archie to meet her from work at the nearby Lyndale Hotel. Unable to get back to their cottage on Tors Road, the young couple had sought shelter with Evelyn’s parents. By now the building was awash and the level was steadily rising as father and son salvaged the week’s takings from the safe. By now their eyes were getting accustomed to the darkness, and they saw the large butcher's block being swept to the back room of the shop. As they scrambled upstairs to their wives and family, the water followed them steadily. It still followed as everybody retreated to the top floor of the building. From here there was no escape for the frightened family as the only window in the attic room was too small to climb through. The next few minutes felt like an eternity. Nervously looking back they saw that the water lapping the top stair had miraculously stopped rising. Later Fred tells of peering through the little window into the darkness and seeing "above me, on the other side of the road, a wall of water as high as the roof itself was pouring along the west side of Shelley's Cottage Hotel and threatening us for a long time that night."

When they all hurried upstairs Freda had managed to grab two small candles as her husband had dropped the torch into the water earlier on. At about 3:30 am the last candle flickered and went out, "It's true," she remembers, "the darkest hour is before dawn." Freda of all people is in a position to say so.

*Summer Cottage.*

Fred mentions he was amazed his little daughter, "had slept soundly, through the noise and crashes that night, in a canvas zip bag that Freda had hurriedly placed her in."

Early next morning after their terrifying ordeal, fireman Michael Sharp appeared at the bedroom window, he was not on a ladder as would be expected at that height, but standing on a mass of boulders twenty five feet high that had buttressed against the building during the night. Returning to their cottage later, they found that it had virtually disappeared. Summer Cottage, their riverside home for six years was never rebuilt for the young family, and the site just behind the East Lyn Hotel was eventually lost to river widening after the flood.

Concern had been aroused in the village at about 7:15 pm when the leat supplying water to the power station was breached and the turbines stopped. Lights in the village dimmed and then went out until Charlie Postles, the engineer, assisted by switchboard attendant Reg Freeman, quickly changed over to the standby diesel generator, which restored power to the villages. By 8 pm the station was awash, although the engineers stood bravely at their post for as long as possible, they were forced to evacuate an hour later. From that moment the village was in complete darkness, other than frequent bolts of lightening which lit a scene that was becoming unrecognisable as the night went on. For their brave action both men were to receive the Queen's Commendation for Brave Conduct in December 1952.

*East Lyn with Tors Road on the left, the power station is the building on the bank on the right. Right picture; inside the power station building.*

At 7:30 pm Police Constables Stanley Pavey and Derek Harper received a telephone call whilst on duty at Lynton police station informing them that high on the moor flooding had washed part of the Simonsbath road away. Another caller said that the East Lyn had risen 20 feet and was blocking the road at Rockford.

Calls were coming in thick and fast; three of the part time firemen of Lynton were summoned by Mrs Cockram to Radsbury Farm three miles away at Ilkerton, which the farmer reported was flooding. Sub Officer Bill Widden, Leading Fireman Ernie Tucker, and Fireman Jack Chubb who had joined the brigade in 1950 set off to aid the worried farmer. On their journey up to the moorland farm they were met with a river of water cascading towards them as torrents carrying debris poured from the moor through gateways onto the lane. On arrival the team found water flooding off the field through the front door into the farmhouse. Rolling up a length of carpet, they diverted the water through a cupboard and out of the back door, they could do no more to help under the circumstances. It was obvious the situation was getting serious and the firemen, anxious to return to Lynton, soon realised that there would be more calls that night. Returning to Barbrook they found the road impassable. Forced to abandon the fire tender, Jack Chubb and Ernie Tucker volunteered to make their way through the rushing water to telephone from a nearby farm. Waist high in water and with arms linked they eventually reached the safety of the farm and were quickly ushered in. As Ernie was giving details to the Fire Station a sudden flash of light lit up the darkened room. He was thrown across the floor amidst a shower of sparks and smoke. Rushing to the aid of his shocked and confused friend, Jack quickly realised that lightning had struck the telephone wires. Ernie soon recovered, but finding themselves marooned, the whole crew was forced to spend the night at the farm. Early next morning they made their way back to Lynton and resumed their much-needed duties aiding other rescuers in Lynmouth. Their fire tender had to be abandoned at Barbrook for a few days.

*Above; Barbrook, the original stone bridge can be seen. Right; Efforts are made to reinstate the crossing after the flood.*

Meanwhile, Lynton's other fire tender had been sent to the hamlet of Bridgeball, three miles from Lynmouth where there was a report that Farley Water was flooding homes. This engine accompanied by Constable Harper could get no further than Hillsford Bridge just above Watersmeet, where they found the bridge destroyed. Attempting a return to Lynton, their journey was halted at Barbrook, where water was rushing over the road bridge making it impossible to cross. The party was cut off between the two Lyn rivers, and while wondering their next move, cries were heard nearby. Miss Winifred Latham, an elderly lady who lived in Bridge House, was trapped in the cellar as water surged through her shop and adjoining home. Constable Harper, Firemen Michael Sharp and Henry Glover, already soaked to the skin, waded into the shop and brought the terrified woman out, leaving her safely with friends whose house was on higher ground. However, the problem of their return to Lynton remained, the time was about 10:30 pm and all were anxious to report to their fire station. PC Harper decided on a precarious attempt to cross the bridge. Roped to the fire-crew, he had struggled just a few yards when a sudden wall of water swiftly bore down the West Lyn toward him. His colleagues hearing the roar pulled him back just in time as the shattered bridge was swept downstream. With all telephone lines down there was nothing to do except wait for the waters to subside before attempting a return to Lynton.

*The site of Bevan's and Vale Cottages.*

It was about 1:45 am when the fire-crew and policeman set off. With the Barbrook bridge gone they would have to go back through Lynmouth, there was no other route available. Making their way slowly down the Watersmeet Road the fire tender was confronted with boulders, trees, and telegraph poles which the valiant crew had to clear as they progressed. It was 3 o'clock in the morning when they finally arrived in Lynmouth, having taken over an hour to travel a mile and a half. Derek Harper recalls, "Our first job was to rescue all persons trapped in houses. The tender had only managed to reach Mansell's Garage as a pile of boulders, trees and wrecked motor cars completely blocked the Watersmeet Road to Lyndale Cross at the centre of the village. This pile I estimated to be sixty yards long by thirty feet high". Within a short time of reaching Lynmouth, Constable Harper and the firemen set about rescuing eight people from a house liable to collapse at any moment. Derek, realising the full scale of what had happened, decided that some communication would have to be made with the outside world, but all telephones in the area were out of action. Joan Taylor, a telephonist at the Barnstaple exchange that night, recalls that the line to Lynton went dead at about 9:15pm. Just previously, she had answered a number of calls from Lynmouth residents. She remembers, "Their voices were in a state of panic as they told of the river eroding its banks as they were talking to me, I could hear a dreadful noise in the background - and then the line went dead".

At about 3:30 am, making his way carefully over the parapet of the wrecked Lyndale Bridge, the brave Lynton Constable made his way up to the Tors Hotel to telephone for help. Major Karol Bruckner, the hotel's owner, informed him that the receiver was silent. By this time 150 people had sought shelter at The Tors and the Constable told them to stay there until help arrived. Borrowing the Major's Hudson Terraplane car, he set off on the A39 with pastry cook Konrandt Plichta, to try and get help at Porlock village 10 miles away.

Standing today at the road-side near the top of Porlock Hill can be seen an old-fashioned black and yellow telephone box that is the only Grade 2 listed AA box in the country. The listing of box No A137 is due to its past history for aiding the many motorists who required assistance ascending the notoriously steep hill. From this box, PC Harper made the call to Superintendent West at Barnstaple Police station informing him of what had happened. It was from this telephone box that news of the Lynmouth tragedy was announced to the world.

*AA box No. A137*

On 21st August, a letter from K J T Bruckner of The Tors Hotel appeared in the Times newspaper. Part of it read; "My wife and members of my staff join me in wishing to place on record the heroic gallantry and devotion to duty shown by Police Constable Harper, of Lynmouth when this village was overwhelmed and devastated last Friday night." In December 1952, Her Majesty Queen Elizabeth II awarded the George Medal to the young village constable.

While the two fire crews had been busy earlier that night, they were unaware that two hundred yards downstream from the wrecked Barbrook bridge, a terrible event had occurred.

Barbrook is a small village lying a mile from the twin resorts on the main road to Barnstaple. As you leave towards Lynton, a memorial garden heads a row of eight semi-detached houses. The little garden stands on the site of the most tragic happening of the Lynmouth flood. Barbrook Cottages were originally twelve council houses built in 1928 with their back gardens standing 30 feet above the West Lyn.

On the fateful night, two Australian girls working as secretaries during their stay in London, were on holiday in North Devon. The girls had been dropped off in Barbrook after getting a lift the nine miles from Blackmoor Gate. The driver had recommended that comfortable lodgings could be had at the home of Mrs. Ridd. Although it was only a short walk, Gwenda Oxley 22, and her friend Joyce Hiscock 21 were wet through when they arrived at No.10 Barbrook Cottage where Emily Ridd lived. She and her 8 year-old grandson Rodney Dimmock, who was staying with her for the weekend, welcomed them in. Emily made sure they quickly changed into some dry clothes that belonged to her daughter. Soon after, the swollen river rose and was surrounding the cottage. Realising the danger Emily decided to seek shelter at her daughter's house in Lynton with Rodney and the two girls. Cautiously they all made their way along the flooded road clinging to a stone wall for support. In the pitch darkness, they did not see a large gap where the river had scoured the wall away. Tragically, none were to survive being swept through the breach into the raging water. Emily's empty cottage collapsed into the river a short time afterwards. Rodney's father George was helping rescuers in Lynmouth early next morning when he was told the dreadful news by PC Harper that cottages at Barbrook had been washed away. Until that moment, he had thought that his young son was safe at the home of his mother-in-law. Although overgrown with foliage, the gap in the wall has never been repaired to this day.

*Joyce Hiscock and Gwenda Oxley on board P&O Oriana at Melbourne in April 1952 before sailing to England*

It is ironic, but earlier in the day Gwenda and Joyce had visited the village of Hartland in the east of North Devon. Mr. & Mrs. Shapland, a couple who had befriended them, had offered an invitation for both to have tea in the Hartland Quay Hotel that afternoon. Both girls politely declined saying they were keen to get to Lynmouth by evening. Their bodies were eventually recovered from the sea and then cremated at Bristol Crematorium. The ashes of the friends who were inseperable in life are buried together in Melbourne's Boxhill cemetery.

As in most close communities, families often live near to each other. Tom Floyd (63) local postman and a respected Lynton councillor lived at No 11 with his wife and 27 year old son Fred. It was about 10 pm when Fred shouted to his father that the river wall was breaking and water filled the back garden. Instantly the house shuddered and the kitchen stove crashed over, also in the house at the time were Tom's daughter Elsie Bowen with husband Ronald, their two sons David (11) and Kenneth (9), and Benjamin and Emma Coult who were on holiday from their home in Durham. As the water poured into the room, a valiant effort was made by the men to save Tom's disabled wife Mary, but without warning the whole house toppled over into the river with all inside. As the building broke up in the thundering waters, Tom somehow managed to surface clinging to a protruding wall. Unable to hold on he was being swept away to certain death when miraculously he was pulled from the torrent by his daughter Ellen Jenkins (36) who lived next door but one at No 9. Ellen told of what happened, "As the water rose outside the door my husband Mansell said it was time to get out. He pushed me out of the door - into a torrent that was up to my thighs". Ellen struggled toward higher ground clasping her baby, 18 month old Brenda, while holding on tightly to her 10-year-old daughter Dilys. She saw her nephews Roy Williams (16) and his brother Maurice (13) floundering nearby. Roy was holding his young brother John (4) in his arms. They lived at No 12 and Roy had been baby-sitting while his parents George and Ivy Williams and Roy's sister Edna (17) were in Lynton for the evening. Luckily there was just enough time for all the youngsters to escape through the window just before their house collapsed into the river.

As all the family struggled on to higher ground, in the dim light Ellen saw a man floating towards her on all fours and almost submerged by the flood. She recalled, "I recognised the grey and red striped shirt of my father, his coat and boots had been torn off. I managed to grab him by the braces as he went past me and I just hung on until we reached safety". Tom was to learn that he had lost his

*The council houses at Barbrook*

*Two buildings were lost - and almost a third.*

wife, his son and daughter, his son-in-law, two grandsons and his home. Only Tim, his Jack Russell terrier, had survived. Twelve people lost their lives from the four homes that had collapsed into the raging West Lyn at Barbrook that night. The body of little Kenneth Bowen was later recovered a mile away at Lynmouth. He was found under the butchers block in Medway's shop on Watersmeet Road. The body of his big brother David was never found. Even today, the memory of what happened that night to this tragic family is still fresh in the mind of the villagers.

*Middleham Cottages*

Due to the confusion, and emotion of people during the flood, it is impossible to confirm the exact timing of events by survivors of that terrible night. What happens in a few minutes can seem like an hour when people are subjected to horror as prolonged as this night was. Another tragedy that was about to unfold started at about 8:15 pm. Middleham was a tidy row of ten cottages backing onto the East Lyn at the head of Lynmouth. Residents noticed the river was just two feet from garden level. By the time they had gone upstairs to look, the river was surrounding their homes. As water started to flood in they realised it was time to evacuate. William Watts (80) and his wife Maud (72) along with her brother Gabriel Litson (78) could not be encouraged to leave their cottage and seek shelter, they assured neighbours that they would be safe upstairs. The elderly residents were not worried, having experienced light flooding of their homes in the past.

Quickly, the rest of this small community gathered a few belongings and together made their way through the rising waters to the empty school. The building was only 50 yds. away but was on slightly higher ground. Some decided to venture on to the village, struggling down Watersmeet Road, which by now had been transformed into a fast flowing stream.

Later those sheltering in the school could see an oil lamp flickering dimly in the only cottage that remained inhabited. An incessant roar of water, the loud rumble of large boulders, the strong smell of damp earth, and the blackness of the night broken by frequent flashes of lightening was with them all night. Worst of all, the uncertainty of what would happen to them was an emotion they and all others in the village that night were experiencing.

It was around 1:30 in the morning as far as can be determined, when those huddled together sheltering in the school heard over the roar of the mayhem around them, an overwhelming noise of crashing boulders and grating stone. Looking out of the window into the pitch-dark moments later, they saw that the little oil lamp had been extinguished. Their worst fears were justified early the next morning. All the cottages had disappeared tragically with their aged occupants and the foundations had been scoured away 10 feet to the riverbed. Swinging in the breeze was a small Bed & Breakfast sign in one of the cottage gardens, all that remained of Middleham. Today, the area looks much as it did the day after the flood.

*Bottom of Lynmouth Hill. The annex to Granville Hotel is on the left.*

Tragedies such as the Lynmouth flood will always bring out deeds of heroism in people - in ordinary people. The inner strength that will try to overcome adversity was shown that night by many, but stories of their valour will sadly remain untold publicly forever.

One of the buildings swept away that night was the Plymouth Brethren chapel that had stood in the centre of the village next to Glen Fruit Shop. Amongst members of the church congregation were Roland Freestone and his wife who kept Cliff House Hotel in Tors Park. Courage shown that night by people acting with little regard to their own safety helping others, can be typified by the actions of their 24 year old son Michael, a Special Constable in the village.

Before the flood there were five more houses at the top of Tors Road than there are today, the woods of Tors Park rise steeply behind this attractive row of cottages facing the East Lyn river. With the floodwater roaring down the road at the front, a high wall and the steep hill at the back, residents,

*Tors Road with the remains of Rose Cottage on the right.*

some of them elderly, were trapped as the water rose in their homes. Michael waded waist deep into a house to rescue a frightened seven-year-old girl who was crying for her parents. Thanks to his action she was soon reunited with her grateful mother and father. He then went to the aid of two elderly people and three girls, guiding them over the roofs of out-buildings to the safety of the hillside. By this time Michael was exhausted, but he realised there were other friends and neighbours whose lives were in peril.

Towards the end of the Tors Road was Victoria Cottage, home of Fred and Nellie Holsgrove who were the parents of Freda Fouracre. Michael helped both through the threatening waters to Inglewood Cottage next door where Dorothy Litson was at home. Only a little later that evening everybody had to evacuate, helped again by the young man, before that cottage also fell victim to the flood. They all eventually spent the night safely at Dean Cottage with Eva Holsgrove a few doors down the road. Very soon afterwards this brave man then showed trapped visitors to a place of refuge amongst the trees. In Rose Cottage at the end of Tors Road lived two elderly ladies, Mrs. Hannah Jarvis (77), and her sister Miss Elizabeth Cannon (75). Both could be seen together in an upstairs room at the front of the house. When Michael looked he could see that the front lower part of the building had collapsed. Above the tumultuous noise he shouted for them to get to the back of the house. His effort was in vain, for as he spoke the whole building, together with the sisters, crumpled into the raging torrent before his eyes. Moments later, there was only the back wall of Rose Cottage remaining. Soon after the flood Michael Freestone left the village and became a policeman with the Brighton police force.

Visitors, who came to Lynmouth and Lynton for their week's holiday, would book to see the variety show in the Pavilion at the foot of the cliff railway. It was their treat on a Friday evening before they went home on the Saturday morning. On the 15th August, the show was "Seaside Notions" starting at 7 o'clock, with popular Scottish comedian, Al Raie, who was down for the season from the Palace Theatre in Bath.

Early on in the performance, a local boatman rushed backstage to tell him the rising water was giving cause for concern. Announcing this message to the audience only a dozen people left as little danger could be seen from where they were, the show continued.

*Lynmouth Pavilion in its heyday*

Later, when the lights went out as the power station failed, performers and audience joined together in a sing-song. Whilst the soprano was singing 'Unforgettable' accompanied by pianist Patricia Kent, the increasingly nervous atmosphere in the Pavilion suddenly broke. Everybody left at once. Performers left quickly wearing only their stage costumes with a coat hurriedly flung over them. Filing out into the pouring rain, they found the esplanade awash, some turned back up the steps and made for Mars Hill which runs high around the back of the village. Others walked towards the harbour to make for their hotels and lodgings. Once around the corner they were met by a river of water flowing down the road towards them. A group of four woman, holiday-makers from London, all linked arms to support themselves as they struggled knee-deep through the fast flowing water to the top of Lynmouth Street. As they turned the corner onto Lynmouth Hill they were met by a torrent of deeper water waist high. Elsie Cherry (56), who was nearest to the swollen river, lost her footing and was swept suddenly away from her friends who were helpless to save her. Rescuers who dragged the surviving women into the Falls Hotel, found one of them unconscious. After recovering she was put to bed, her cries and sobbing for her lost friend were heard throughout the night. On the 6th October Elsie's body was found on the beach at Clovelly, forty miles down the coast.

Carl Shaw, the producer of the concert that night, wrote from London on September 14th to the local council asking if he could collect material and a billboard that had been left outside the Pavilion during the confusion that night. Leonard Ridge, the Town Clerk replied that his possessions left inside the theatre could be reclaimed at any time, but not his billboard that was left at the bottom of the steps. He explained that it was probably now floating around somewhere in the middle of the Bristol Channel.

Guy Litson (14) and his younger brother Andrew (10) left the performance with their father Cecil who had arrived showing concern for his son's safety. Father and sons started to make their way back along Mars Hill in the pouring rain until they drew near to their home behind the Lyndale Hotel. As they came to Sheppards newsagent shop on Watersmeet Road they found holiday-maker, Harold Summerville, trapped in the doorway. By now it was impossible for the little party to struggle on through the rising water and Guy impulsively smashed a window to gain refuge. The four 'burglars' were confronted by a very irate Amy Sheppard and her daughter Florence, who soon turned their concern to a stock of postcards floating all around the shop. "Pick them up, pick them up!" Mrs. Sheppard shrieked, showing more concern for postcards than the welfare of her unexpected guests. Her mood soon mellowed when the seriousness of the situation was realised and everyone retreated upstairs as the water continued to rise.

Adding to the terrifying ordeal that the boys were going through that night, was the constant worry of where their mother was. Mrs.Betty Litson worked at the Lyndale Hotel and was on duty that evening. Unbeknown to the boys and their father, she was trapped in the hotel with 44 guests and other members of staff and spent the night showing equal worry for her husband and sons. Early next morning the rain had stopped but there was an uneasy calm. Emerging from the ruined building onto the mass of boulders that lay all around, the shock of seeing their wrecked home and village was made up for when there was a tearful but joyful reunion of the family in the battered hotel. Amidst the excitement, young Andrew asked if he could use the hotel toilet nearby, returning eagerly to his mother soon after. Almost immediately the pounding received by the building all night from the two rivers became apparent on the structure. There was a loud crack, a shudder, and a large section of the Lyndale Hotel slowly collapsed into a pile of rubble, including the toilet the little boy had used just a minute before. Thankfully, nobody was injured. Miraculously the two boys and their parents had all survived, but sadly they were unaware that two elder members of the Litson family had been lost during the night.

Harry Litson was the village taxi driver who lived at Inglewood Cottage where Fred and Nellie Holsgrove had been sheltering. Harry had popped into the Rising Sun for a drink at the end of the day having left his taxi outside the nearby lifeboat house. Showing concern at the rising river, he left his friends at about 7pm to return home. By now there were many frightened people needing help throughout the village. Harry was last seen with others helping rescue some of those trapped at Priors Cottage in Lynmouth Street. Nobody saw him being swept away, but that night the community lost a well-loved friend and a popular councillor.

Nothing was spared as the torrent of water poured off the moor and thundered uncontrollably down the rivers to the village. Many newly created streams rushed down the steep valley sides adding to the awesome volume of water the narrow valley was already carrying.

Sheep, cows, Exmoor ponies and farm animals stood no chance of escape as they were swept off their feet into the catastrophic flow.

Three days after the flood the carcass of a stag was washed onto the beach at Westward Ho! thirty miles down the coast. Even this proud and fleeting Exmoor beast had been unable to escape the deluge that fell on the higher slopes of the moor that night.

A peculiar fact of the flood was that the buildings were not damaged, or swept away in sequence

*East Lyn. Watersmeet Road (bottom of picture) is filled with debris.*

through the village. Some in the centre of Lynmouth were lost earlier than properties further up the river. Picturesque Woodside Hotel, the first building met by the flood in the Watersmeet valley, sustained very little damage, yet at Middleham, 200 metres downstream and on the opposite bank, nothing remained of the ten cottages, not even the foundations.

*It is hard to imagine the strength of a flood that completely destroyed Vale and Bevan's Cottages.*

*Gwen Richards with her sons Bernard and Earnest on the day of the baby's christening - shortly before the disaster.*

A footpath along the bank of the East Lyn from the Lyndale Hotel led to an area called The Ham. At this point there was a row of four council houses facing the river. Bevan's Cottages were built in 1936 and were adjacent to a small row of three called Vale Cottages. Just before 10 o'clock, water started to flood into the homes. One of the residents was Fred Bale who was a well-known character of the village. Driving down Countisbury Hill into Lynmouth he was usually the first villager you would meet. Standing in the middle of the road at busy Lyndale Cross directing traffic and guiding visitors, he always dressed in a large white coat with white gloves and cap, even on a hot summer day. Water poured through his front door when a tree smashed it open cutting off any escape from that side of the cottage. Fred, his wife Dolly and his two young daughters, Jean and Beryl, scrambled upstairs and made their way through a bedroom window onto the roof of an adjoining garage and so to the comparative safety of the Watersmeet Road.

Meanwhile, most residents in Bevan's Cottages were evacuating quickly. Charles Litson, an elderly veteran of the Great War was lucky to get out in time considering the leg injury he had suffered in the conflict. It was his brother Gabriel who was to lose his life at Middleham later that night.

The level was rising fast as Charles and his wife, Ann, along with neighbours scrambled to higher ground at the end of their back gardens. Suddenly a shout was heard from No. 3 and looking back their friend Bill Richards was seen desperately calling for help from an upstairs window. Within minutes, before any aid could be given the whole row of seven cottages disappeared entirely. Bill (30), his wife Gwendolene (32), their sons Bernard (3), and Ernest (3 months) were a young family who were all so tragically lost.

John Pedder, a teenager and keen angler, had come home early to Lynton after fishing because of the heavy rain that afternoon. Early that evening his father Jack, a local councillor and Lynmouth postmaster, had heard there was flooding down in the village and asked if John would come with him to Lynmouth. Hurrying down, they eventually reached the post office in Lynmouth Street. On arrival, assistance was given to three frightened young women found huddled together on the Post Office steps. The women had been trying to escape from the swollen river that was flowing down the street. On entering the shop, Jack immediately began to salvage account books and money from the safe. Suddenly a side door of the building burst open under the water pressure

*Lynmouth Street showing the post office on the right.*

sweeping a large tree into the post office that trapped them in a corner. "My son smashed a skylight, climbed up on the roof, and hauled me up just as the steps I was standing on was washed away." said Mr. Pedder. After their narrow escape, father and son gave assistance rescuing people from the cliff behind the post office. Later, a tremendous crashing noise was heard in the distance. "The Rhenish Tower has gone!" said John, "Never." replied his father, "If the tower has gone then so has Lynmouth." Next morning his prophetic words were to be confirmed. In later life, John followed in the family tradition by becoming Mayor and Lynmouth postmaster. His grandfather as postmaster in January 1899 had received the telegraph message of a ship in distress at Porlock that had led to the famous lifeboat launch mentioned later.

Phlip Nichols was tidying the caravan she was temporarily living in with her young daughter. The caravan was sited on the Glen Lyn estate near the West Lyn river. Phlip recalls looking out of the window and seeing the water washing near to the caravan. "I grabbed a few things, picked up my daughter and hurried around to the Bonnicott Hotel." She remembers, "During the night we all heard loud shouting over the terrible noise as a row of cottages nearby was washed away." (This would have been Bevan's Cottages). "Early in the morning it was realised there was no water supply to the hotel and everybody was desperate for a cup of tea." Phlip remembered she had left two water containers outside of her caravan and made her way back to retrieve them. Although shocked by the devastation that lay all around, the little things stick in her mind. "I'll always remember the title of a sodden paperback I saw lying in the mud, probably washed from the cottages at Barbrook," she says, "it was a novel called *The Dark Waters*."

*A wrecked Ford motor car, one of many vehicles lost that night.*

An unusual sight in the village that people recall, were the motor cars caught in the flood rolling around in the flow and out to sea with headlights on. The eerie glow in the darkness made them look like wallowing sea monsters. Water had, of course, shorted the electric circuits.

*Boulders washed down by the West Lyn, some weighing 50 tons.*

*Lyn River with Nelson's Tea Gardens on the right.*

*The torrent diverted by an outcrop of rock, left buildings at the lower end of Lynmouth unscathed.*

*Normally flowing between the buildings on the right, the West Lyn diverted and joined the East Lyn at Lyndale Bridge.*

## Rescue

As you travel down the steep hill from Lynton to it's twin village today, you are met by a sweeping bend at the bottom. Over the large retaining wall, an abutment in a garden is all that remains of the impressive Lyn Valley Hotel. On the night, the West Lyn ripped away the Northeast section of the building, including the imposing tower. This section of the hotel crashed down at approximately 11pm, as far as can be ascertained. The loss of two members of staff could have been at this time, but nobody saw Stella Bates and Jessie Whitbread disappear. The two women were from Bedford and had come to the hotel to work during the summer season. It was at this time that a section of the West Lyn Hotel opposite, was swept away taking the life of the cook Ada Barwick as it crumbled into the thundering waters.

Noise of the hotel stonework falling drew the attention of a team of rescuers working nearby. They realised they would have difficulty reaching the hotel as deep fast moving torrents surrounded it, making access to the marooned people from the ground impossible. Stan Clapperton, a porter at the hotel, managed to gain access through the kitchen door. As he did a terrific rush of water enveloped the ground floor of the building. There were about 50 people trapped in the hotel. Ushering everybody to the top floor, he shouted to his fellow rescuers to fetch a ladder from his nearby home. A long ladder was slung from the retaining wall high above the rear of the hotel, across Granny's Lane, to a bedroom window. It was a very dangerous method of escape, but there was no alternative. One at a time, tied to a rope, each person crawled precariously across the ladder to safety. Throughout the night, torch light flashes piercing the pitch-blackness, showed where people were signalling their desperate plight. It was useless for them to shout above the noise of roaring water and crashing debris. The Smith family were trapped in their home at Priors Cottage by more than 4 feet of water rushing down Lynmouth Street. Tom Richards threw a rope from the roof of Chapman's shoe shop opposite and tied it fast to a street lamp. Men of the village then safely evacuated John Smith, his wife Myra and his daughter Jenny, along with five guests staying at the house including Myra's 85 year old mother. It was a dangerous rescue as the men holding the rope waded through the swirling water with those rescued clinging to their backs. They were taken to the Bath Hotel where refuge was given until later that morning. One member of the rescue team who worked steadily throughout the night was Dr Manners P. Nightingale, the local GP. He had been called out at 9.20 pm on Friday evening and worked ceaselessly with rescuers until 3.30 am the following morning. At that time the flooding had receded but he was still walking alone knee deep in mud and water up Lynmouth Street finally checking to see that everyone was safe.

*The Beach Hotel*

Rescuers, who had aided the residents of the Lyn Valley hotel with their ladders, were able to apply the same method of help to those trapped in the Bath Hotel further down the street. Although this hotel flooded badly it did not suffer structural damage. Residents and staff were evacuated by ladder to the safety of Mars Hill behind the hotel. Next door to the Bath, Phyllis Bigg, manageress of the Beach Hotel firmly took charge of her thirteen guests when the hotel started to flood. "Upstairs" she ordered them, but the water followed quickly, catching up with them on the second floor. Everybody clambered out through a bedroom window onto the roof. Marooned and huddled together with noise and commotion below them, they sang hymns to keep spirits up: "O God our help in ages past our hope for years to come, Our shelter from the stormy blast...." Indeed, help did come from above. A rescue team positioned a ladder from Mars Hill to the roof of the hotel enabling all to climb up to safety. Soon after, the torrent swept the hotel completely away. Sited next to the Beach Hotel facing the harbour was the lifeboat house. Although no lifeboat had been stationed there since 1944, (this part of the coastline was well catered for by Ilfracombe and Minehead lifeboat stations) upstairs was the Village Institute. By early light all that remained was a wall with a large door hanging from a single hinge.

*Remains of the lifeboat house*

The loss of this building was

especially sad, as it had been the scene of the most famous rescue in the history of the Lifeboat Institute fifty-three years before.

> On the 12th January 1899 a call was made to aid a boat in distress off Porlock Weir in Somerset. Unable to launch at Lynmouth because of the force 8 gale, Jack Crocombe, the coxswain, shouted an instruction that has gone down in the annals of lifeboat history, "We'll launch from Porlock". Crew and villagers helped the horses with lifeboat in tow, climb the steep two-mile long Countisbury Hill, and travel the thirteen miles across Exmoor to Porlock in atrocious weather. Finishing their adventurous journey down Porlock Hill, they launched the "Louisa" on the beach at Porlock Weir, ten hours after leaving Lynmouth. The "Forrest Hall" and crew were saved. On the 12th January 1999, a memorable re-enactment of the event took place over the same route.

Considering the damage to the lifeboat house, it is amazing that Manor Cottage next door was hardly touched by the flood waters. There is a simple explanation. Looking at pre-1952 photographs of Lynmouth, it is seen that the harbour wall is built on top of a large outcrop of rock in front of the lifeboat house (page 95). *Turbal Rock* still exists, but is now under the widened road in front of the Flood Memorial Hall in Lynmouth. Coupled with a natural cliff protrusion behind Manor cottage, the waters were diverted away from the lower end of the village where only light damage was caused to buildings. Sadly, this diversion was aimed directly at Lynmouth's famous landmark, the Rhenish Tower, that overlooked the harbour. This solid structure that had withstood the onslaught of the sea since 1832, was gone completely the next morning. Strangely, the council deckchairs that were kept alongside the tower, still stood neatly stacked in position the next day alongside a row of boards advertising boat trips due to sail. Five days after the flood two deckchairs were found on a beach thirty miles away. A Westward Ho! resident used them in his garden for many years, still with LUDC indelibly marked on them.

## Morning After

At first light on the Saturday morning when the village of Lynton began to stir, most residents awoke feeling relieved that the rain had stopped. Holiday-makers would be happier and trade may be a little brisker. Saturday was "changeover" day, when visitors would be doing their last minute shopping before they travelled home. An influx of new guests would be starting to arrive by early afternoon. The air of optimism was soon cut short as news of their neighbours in the village below spread throughout the little town. Word travels quickly in small communities. Although the previous day's rain had caused local flooding in parts of the town, nothing would prepare them for the shock that was to come to them from the little village 500 feet below. Some immediately made their way eagerly down the hill, concerned about relatives or friends but not really knowing what to expect. A smell of damp earth mixed with acrid sewage grew stronger as they hurried down the steep path, overwhelming them as they neared the village. Glimpses of an unfamiliar scene were caught through the trees. The feelings that overcame them when they arrived were emotions that few people ever experience. Sheer disbelief at what lay before them, a mass of boulders and broken trees everywhere, covering the sites of buildings they had known all their lives. Enormous boulders choking the course of the river, the river itself flowing through a high self-made valley of stone and debris that covered the heart of their sister village. A damp muddy line showing where the water level had reached up to the word "Hotel" high along the cream painted face of the Lyndale Hotel, the battered building still standing proudly amidst the ruins surrounding it. Damp remnants of clothing that had been caught high on the branches of riverside trees. Missing walls of the Lyn Valley Hotel giving it the appearance of a discarded open doll's house with tilting beds and furniture ready to slide onto the rubble filling the street below.

The East Lyn, now three times wider than it should be with an unfamiliar shape of bare new riverbanks scoured and stripped of greenery.

Stunned villagers were clustered on either side of the bank marooned from each other by the wrecked bridges. Although river levels had dropped, the water still tumbled noisily as two groups sent eagerly awaited news of their neighbours fate across the river scribbled on notes attached to a length of twine. Behind the Lyndale Hotel lay an area of sodden desolation where yesterday a row of cottages with their neatly tended gardens had stood.

The familiar sight of large chestnut trees that on the day before had shaded the little lane beside the river leading to Sunnyside. Now there were no chestnut trees, there was no lane.

They were bewildered as their eyes looked towards the lower end of the village. It was high tide and a threatening lake of sea covered the whole area, unhindered now by the loss of the solid harbour wall. Where were the Beach Hotel, the lifeboat house and the famous Rhenish Tower that had withstood the sea for 120 years? Before them lay an unrecognisable view of the harbour they had known and loved all their lives. At least the Rising Sun and esplanade had remained intact, although these buildings were now marooned from the rest of the village with the harbour road gone completely. Around the corner, the 62-year-old cliff railway was complete and undamaged because of it's protected position on the esplanade. In fact, after a thorough inspection, it proved to be of valuable help, serving as a lifeline between the two villages after the flood. There were people around, a lot of people, some were holiday-makers climbing from bedroom windows onto ladders put up by rescuers who were helping them down. They were being led to the bottom of Lynmouth Hill carrying their suitcases and any belongings they may have salvaged. The only access from the hill into Lynmouth was by a ladder dropped down to the back of Granny's Lane, which still runs its original route behind the post office. A cluster of dazed survivors was mustering at Prospect Corner. Bob Jones, a local builder had driven his lorry down at 4:30 in the morning and was taking people back up the hill to the safety of Lynton. Later, as more were being rescued from the wrecked buildings, a bus was called in to help with the evacuation. In all, about 700 survivors were taken to Lynton. As the tide ebbed, an amazing view unfolded; the foreshore was covered with the wreckage of the night. The whole bay was littered with wood and stone from the shattered buildings. Broken furniture mixed with the remnants of somebody's cooking stove, twisted and unrecognisable motor cars, some still with air in the tyres. Bent lamp posts, broken telephone poles, smashed crockery, toys, ripped books, shattered petrol pumps, and the sight of trees dotted around the shore, standing upright where the roots had wedged in the rocky beach giving the impression of a petrified forest. This mass of shattered floating debris was to ebb and flow with the changing tides of Lynmouth Bay for many days to come.

*Bottom of Lynmouth Hill the morning after.*

Fishermen and pleasure-boat owners had watched helplessly as all nineteen craft in the harbour were swept out to sea where they sank or were wrecked on the foreshore. “My life savings went into my boats, now they are all gone,” said Ken Oxenham who had lost three craft. One was a trawler worth £2,000, a considerable amount of money in 1952, a house could be bought then for far less. “Like so many others, I have to start from scratch. But I have to be glad that I still have my skin”. All that remains of Ken’s boat today is the salvaged brass bell inscribed with the vessel’s name, “Grateful”.

Later it was realised two large petrol storage tanks that had been under the forecourt of the Glen Lyn filling station had been scoured from their deep site at the bottom of Lynmouth Hill. They were never seen again, just as the garage they came from - was never seen again.

On the East Lyn about a mile upstream from Lynmouth had stood a small Edwardian factory. Lynrock Mineral Water Company had been established in the early 20th century bottling natural water that issued from a spring on the riverbank. As in the power station, water from the river was utilised to power the bottling plant by a hydroelectric system. The spring water was claimed to be beneficial for the treatment of many human ailments, giving it a national reputation as an aid to a healthy life. This claim is surprising since the water was advertised to have ‘radioactive’ properties, obviously the word had a different significance during the 1920s. Although the factory was not in use at the time of the flood, the spring had refreshed many over the years on their walk up to Watersmeet. This sturdy little building was completely washed away along with the site and its substantial river retaining wall. Just the spring itself and a section of the wall standing in the river remain today.

*Lynrock Mineral Water Company*

## Help Arrives

Devon County surveyor, Mr. Robert Black Carnegie C.B.E. had arrived at 9:30 am on Saturday morning, after arranging for 100 council workers to be sent to the area from all over North Devon. By lunchtime, they had all arrived, setting to work immediately with colleagues from Lynton Urban District Council. Mrs. Dorothy Slater, Chairman of Lynton Council, called for an emergency council meeting in Lynton Town Hall at twelve noon, but not all could attend. Tom Bevan had spent the terrible night marooned in his Lyndale Hotel looking after forty-four of his guests and staff. Tom Floyd, whose tragic story has been told, and Harry Litson the local taxi driver, who had lost his life while helping to rescue others. Nearly all present had spent the night endeavouring to cope with the unreal happenings of their village. Mr. Carnegie addressed the meeting, "Madam Chairman and gentlemen, this is a national disaster". He was so right. During the meeting responsibility and organisation came to the fore that would have done a large city council proud, let alone representatives of a small Devon village. A second meeting was held on the Sunday morning when Lord Lieutenant of Devon Earl Fortescue, and Lady Fortescue, Brigadier C.H.M. Peto Member of Parliament for North Devon, Lieut. Colonel R.R.M. Bacon Chief Constable of Devon, and Major General C.L.Firbank General Officer Commanding South Western District, attended representing the Army. Leonard Ridge, the Town Clerk was on holiday and rushed back with his wife as soon as he heard of the disaster. All these people and many others started to bring some semblance of order to the chaos around. The long-winded route of red tape that surrounds various authorities and decisions was cut efficiently but democratically by all concerned.

*Barbara Eyres leaves the Lyndale Hotel on Saturday morning. She had been swept from her home the night before.*

People in Lynton gave some of those villagers who had been left homeless refuge, others were given shelter at the Jubilee Hall in Burville Street, which was quickly fitted out as a relief centre. Along the coast at Minehead, the Regal cinema was turned into a refuge taking in those who had lived on the Countisbury side of Lynmouth. Villagers donated clothes, and all the little necessities to make their friends comfortable. We should remember that many survivors escaped with only the clothes they were wearing at the time. Personal possessions of some survivors living today only date from August 1952.

When BBC radio first broke news of the disaster at 7 o'clock on the Saturday morning, a stunned nation reacted quickly. Lynton Town Hall was inundated as offers of help started to pour in from all over the country. Clothes, bedding, blankets, food, volunteers offering their services. The British tradition of rallying around in a time of crisis was upheld throughout the land. Mr. K.W. Greenwood the Sanitary Inspector with Swanage District Council offered to spend his fortnight's holiday at his own expense, helping with any problems for which his profession could be used.

*Evacuating the Lyndale Hotel on Saturday morning.*

By lunchtime on the Monday morning, the appeal for clothes and bedding was fulfiled; special convoys were rushed to the village from the Ministry of Food in London. The Red Cross sent a lorry load of clothes from London which in those days was a long journey by road, as Britain's first motorway was not to open until 1958. Wholesale grocers in Barnstaple kindly sent two and a half tons of food, still rationed from the war. Local hospitals donated 200 pairs of pyjamas. Many churches throughout the country held prayers and took collections for the relief fund, which had been started by the Lord-Lieutenant of the county.

Some holiday-makers in the village at the time were left stranded and penniless, but a National Insurance office was quickly established in Lynton Town Hall to help. During the early 1950s, most people would take cash with them on holiday, credit cards were not in use . Hotel safes which had been swept away contained guests' money and valuables.

This service was also of great benefit to most of the villagers for every business had been affected, suddenly throwing all owners and employees out of work. Arrangements were made to get shocked visitors home, although some wished to continue with their holiday. Hotels at Princetown on Dartmoor offered to cater for them and a party of 14 were picked up on the Monday morning and arrived during the afternoon.

More council workmen from all over Devon and Somerset were brought in to clear the roads and pathways of the debris that choked the village. Private contractors with heavy plant arrived to work alongside council workers.

*PC Derek Harper holding the microphone to the radio strapped to his back, the only communication with the outside world for some time.*

Army units with specialised equipment were quickly drafted in from a wide area. Health workers and nurses promptly arrived to help. Strangely, nobody had sought medical assistance on the night of the flood, but the influx of helpers arriving were to find their services invaluable during the month they stayed. Besides, sewerage pipes had broken and lay exposed all over the village necessitating boiling drinking water, where it was available. Firemen sprayed the streets with disinfectant to guard against any outbreak of disease. RAF and Army units arrived with 700-gallon tanks to supply fresh drinking water. Administering their wise advice, the medical profession safely guarded all from the threat of contamination during their stay in the village. St John Ambulance Brigade set up a central First Aid Post at the bottom of Lynmouth Hill, administering to over 300 minor injuries during their month's occupation.

Billeting the large number of personnel arriving was difficult considering the stricken state of Lynmouth. Personnel were mostly accommodated in Lynton, the Royal Engineers set up headquarters at the Royal Castle Hotel, a camp was erected in Bottom Meadow Car Park including workshops and all facilities that may be needed, the Imperial Hotel was also used by an Army unit. Devon County Council set up temporary headquarters at the Royal Castle hotel working alongside the Royal Engineers. Lynton Town Hall came into its own when established as the main centre for operations under the capable guidance of Leonard Ridge. All manner of Services and Organisations began to descend on the tiny resort, including units from the Army, RAF, British Red Cross, Civil Defence, Women's Voluntary Service, RSPCA, RAC, AA, and many others offering their help.

The strength of the human spirit was shown by both individual and team effort as they helped to ease the predicament of those suffering. Virtually all those who came to help in the aftermath of the flood faced problems that they had not met before. There had been many more volunteers than the thousand people who eventually came from far and near to help clear up and resume order to the village. During the time that they were resident in the resort, their work was carried out with willingness, determination and a lack of fuss that earned the admiration of all local people.

*A brand new motor car balances precariously where the flood left it on Lyndale Bridge.*

The Salvation Army moved in with mobile canteens manned by volunteers from all over Southern England, one travelling from London to help. These became meeting places where people would take a welcome respite from their toil chatting amongst themselves before getting on with the task in hand.

Motoring organisations were quickly on the scene to help with the needs of the many motorists who had come to grief. There is a post flood photograph of a battered Jowett Javelin motor car perched on the parapet of the wrecked Lyndale Bridge, the bonnet is up because the concerned owner had

*Local garages were kept busy retrieving wrecked cars.*

asked an AA patrolman if the car could be checked over as he wished to drive it home! Living up to the reputation of the Association for service, the patrolman obligingly looked all over the obviously wrecked motor car and duly answered with a slow shake of his head.

Both motoring services organised the identification of the many vehicles littering the area. Eventually, 121 were recovered in various states of repair. Twenty-eight motor vehicles were found wrecked, twenty-four badly damaged, most beyond repair, and a total of thirty-eight were never recovered. Army frogmen inspected those further out in the channel in case bodies were trapped inside, thankfully they returned each time saying that all was well.

For all the outstanding service both RAC and the AA organisations did to help stranded motorists, it is ironic that Patrolman Groves had parked his RAC combination in Mansell's garage yard overnight. His Norton motor cycle and sidecar JGJ 408 was swept away from the site off Watersmeet Road, never to be seen again.

From the original document compiled by the RAC two days after the flood, a list of motor vehicles reported missing totals 165 in all. From this list only two vehicles are of foreign manufacture, a Citroen and an American Chrysler, how motoring has changed compared with the amount of British cars on the road today. The list mentions that a Vauxhall DOB 754 belonging to Mr. Field of Birmingham was brought up on the cliff railway. This was because the esplanade area of Lynmouth was left isolated from the rest of the village after the flood. A total of six stranded motor cars were transported up to Lynton by first removing the carriage section from the trolley of the railway.

Many cars were left marooned in the area after bridges had been swept away, their owners returning to Devon some time later to retrieve and drive the vehicles home along one of the 110 roads and lanes that had been repaired after damage. Some owners were not as lucky, the Hillman Minx, registration number AJX 990 belonging to Mr. C.G. Streeter of Halifax is listed as a "Complete wreck, found at low water, not recovered", there were many others in the same condition.

Initially, nobody was sure how many people were missing after the flood, at least thirty, and possibly fifty. Out of the final total of thirty-four souls lost, eleven were people on holiday, including four children. A RAF launch along with other boats cruised the Bristol Channel looking for any sign of bodies. Much of the wooded Exmoor coastline was inaccessible, and on one occasion Constable Harper bravely descended a 700-feet cliff searching for those who had perished.

There was the harrowing scene of a little boat scraping ashore with four of Lynton's part time firemen aboard. They climbed slowly out of the dinghy and with heads bowed, silently stretchered a sad covered form up the stony beach to a waiting St John's ambulance.

*Cars parked awaiting the insurance assessors.*

Early on Saturday morning, Roy Pugsley a young builder from Lynton was helping with other villagers to bring some sense of order to the wreckage around them. Moving on later at about 11-30 am with his father to Nelson's Cottage Tea-room, (so called because a descendant of Lord Nelson had stayed there in 1841) he was upstairs salvaging some personal effects for the owner, Mrs. Cleeva Loosemore. Having made a couple of visits for various items he was in the north wing of the building when his father called up to him. As he moved toward the stairs to answer, the whole wing of the building weakened by the flood twelve hours before, collapsed behind him into the river, leaving an uninterrupted view out to sea. It was a close call for young Roy! The tea-room still survives, the north wing doesn't.

*An excavator clears debris reaching to the first floor of buildings in Watersmeet Road.*

*A local bus is safely retrieved from the Manor grounds. Mr Mansell lost two buses in the flood.*

## Emergency Repairs

*Field Marshall Slim arrives by helicopter at Bottom Meadow in Lynton to direct army relief operations.*

In the evening of Saturday the 16th, the Chief Constable closed the village to all unauthorised persons. Besides the fear of looting, sightseers would hinder the work of those helping to clear up. The greatest fear was the danger of disease from the shattered sewer pipes lying exposed throughout the village. Road-blocks were set up on all routes to the village to keep out anybody who had no good reason to enter the area. Policemen escorted survivors back to try and salvage any belongings they could find in the wreckage of their homes and hotels. On the Saturday morning policemen had stumbled over the debris checking each building for occupants and arranging their move from the village. By evening the evacuation was complete, or so they thought! On Sunday morning, workmen found two elderly sisters still residing in their home at Lyncliff Cottage on the Watersmeet Road. Miss Mary Crocombe (78) and her sister Alice (68) had gone to bed early on the Friday evening and had slept peacefully through the night. Looking around them on the Saturday morning they "thought they had gone potty", but carried on regardless. Alice said when found "if the police knocked on our door, well we didn't hear them, we thought evacuation was optional but we don't want to give the police any more trouble than they have, so reluctantly we shall go ".

Saturday had been a day of 'mend and make do'. It was paramount to get the essential services working again, at least temporarily. Post Office engineers soon established a telephone link with Lynton by early afternoon, and late that night had re-connected lines to all surviving properties in Lynmouth. An incredible feat when considering the damage suffered by the system. All lines were connected to a small automatic exchange in Lynton where the main cable carried them to Barnstaple.

*A Military policeman guards the village on Sunday.*

*Some of the workers brought in to help with emergency repairs.*

The South Western Electricity board was quickly on the scene and within two days had installed a temporary electricity supply. By the 21st August a team of 21 electricians and workers had restored full power to the village and surrounding area. The power station that had supplied the two villages since 1890 was only the second public hydroelectric scheme to be built in Britain. At the time, it was the largest in the country and it continued supplying 100 volts to all homes in the area until the night of the flood. After the National Grid was formed in 1948, virtually the whole of Britain was supplied with a 230 volt system. With the loss of the power station, Lynton and Lynmouth adopted this voltage soon after the flood when they joined the national supply, the last village in the country to do so. It meant, of course, that every light bulb and electrical appliance in both villages that had been supplied by the historic power station was of no use with the new supply voltage. All electrical equipment was replaced in each household and business when the conversion took place.

*With bridges swept away, lorries bringing heavy equipment were forced to negotiate the narrow streets of Lynton.*

*The steep hills leading to Lynmouth caused a number of accidents.*

Heavy equipment was obviously needed to clear the vast amount of debris that covered the village. At depots throughout the country Army units were already organising the supply of excavators, bulldozers, and earth moving equipment, some complete with trailer weighing up to 50 tons. The arrival of these monster trucks would need careful planning, as the only way into Lynmouth was down the narrow Lynmouth Hill, no vehicle of this size had ever negotiated the 1 in 4 gradient. It took an hour for each Scammel lorry and equipment to negotiate the 700 yard (646m) hill, entering the village at night to save interrupting the many activities of the day.

Whenever a disaster occurs we do not always think of the less obvious groups or societies that quickly lends aid to the victims. Such a society that acted immediately was the R.S.P.C.A. They sent Mr. Norton with an ambulance from London to help Inspectors Ambrose and Pickett who had rushed up from Exeter. Chief Inspector Best and Inspector Barr also travelled up from Bournemouth to help their colleagues. Within a short time of their arrival this dedicated team had rescued over 100 domestic and farm animals, including one tortoise and three goldfish. Donald Groves and his wife were forced to leave their Pekinese dogs behind when Myrtle Cottage on Tors Road suddenly started to flood. Two days later whining was heard from inside the property, Inspector John Ambrose clambered over the debris of the flooded cottage and found Ruby, Butterfly, and Peekie, bedraggled but safely huddling together under a broken settee in a downstairs room.

*Some boulders needed two powerful excavators to remove them.*

*A Ruston Bucyrus excavator broke down and was marooned for three high tides.*

Shortly after the disaster, the Society awarded a medal to a very brave young woman. Jennifer Pearce, aged 11, whose parents kept Orchard House Hotel in Lynmouth, had successfully fought her way through the rising water to save her pony, which was tethered in a stable behind the Lyndale Hotel. Exhausted and against all odds, the little girl led her animal through deep swirling water to the safety of higher ground.

Within a couple of days Lynmouth was a hive of activity with approximately a thousand soldiers and workers covering many trades. Some of the boulders that been swept down the West Lyn were too large to lift, even with the heavy equipment that had arrived. Army sappers carefully blew up some weighing as much as 50 tons on site.

In total, 114,000 tons of miscellaneous debris was eventually cleared from the village after the flood. Many tons of this material was quickly used to reconstitute the riverbanks that had been badly scoured especially where the rivers met near the Lyndale Bridge. Large amounts of rubble were also used to reinforce sea defenses on the east beach. The Manor esplanade is now only 4 feet (1.2m) above the beach compared with 22 feet (6.7m) before the flood.

On rare occasions during winter storms, the sea displaces rocks to expose the rusty remains of wrecked motor cars deposited on the beach at that time.

One of the main priorities was to replace the road bridges that had been lost. Bailey bridges used so successfully during the Second World War came into their own in these circumstances. Men of the 121 Army Engineers (TA) had a bridge erected at Barbrook by the following Saturday, giving much easier access to the village. Later, a similar bridge was laid at Hillsford Bridge near Watersmeet, both river crossings giving valuable service until permanent bridges had been built a couple of years later.

*Harbour defenses are quickly constructed before the high tide due in September.*

Normally when armed services are brought in on a peacetime exercise the Commander of the unit involved directs them. On this occasion it was decided that all service personnel would be working under the direction of the County Surveyor Mr. Carnegie. As he was also surveyor of the Devon River Board, Mr. Carnegie was in a position to make immediate decisions when needed. Among the list of seemingly impossible problems that were faced by all, another threat from water was suddenly realised. The harbour wall was in ruins and an exceptional high tide was due in early September, only two weeks away. Lynmouth would be threatened again, only this time by the sea and the lower end of the village was especially vulnerable with no sea defenses remaining. Nine hundred men of the 6th Training Battalion R.A.S.C. were mobilised to the task. Utilising timber salvaged from the beach and materials found in the village itself, the men worked ceaselessly to build a temporary wall. Their effort was not in vain, and Lynmouth was saved the trauma of being flooded a second time.

All army units had moved out of Lynmouth by September 11th after carrying out such a variety of works, it would be impossible to list them all. Their help alongside civil contractors laying pipes, building bridges, clearing debris from the streets and riverbed, is a debt that Lynmouth will always appreciate. Their enthusiasm and professional attitude to the work they carried out while in the village, was of incalculable value. They and the many people who laboured day and night were the reason that Lynmouth was quickly reopened to the public exactly one month after the disaster. In total, nineteen army units with their various skills had quickly helped bring invaluable order to the village.

It was a beautiful day when Mrs Dorothy Slater, Chairman of Lynton Urban District Council, raised the Union Flag on a flagpole near the Lyndale Hotel at noon on Saturday 16th September. This woman had worked ceaselessly for the community and thoroughly deserved the Order of the British Empire awarded to her in the following New Year Honours' List. The first vehicle to drive into Lynmouth was a lorry which had been waiting patiently on Countisbury Hill for the village to re-open. It drove slowly over Lyndale Bridge to loud cheers with its welcome load of beer barrels.

Emergency work expenditure had totalled £74,293 4s 11p of which the Government Exchequer granted £57,500.

*The Lyn Valley Hotel was the last building to be demolished. The centre of this picture shows the width of the original Prospect Bridge.*

*The Lyndale Hotel was finally demolished by Blackford contractors on August Bank Holiday 1954.*

*Rebuilding the famous Rhenish Tower, August 1954.*

## Appeal

Earl Fortesque Lord Lieutenant of Devon and Lord Hilton, who held a similar position for Somerset, launched an appeal for the flood victims on 17th August. The response from the public was immediate.

Her Majesty Queen Elizabeth sent a message of deepest sympathy and made a "handsome donation" to the fund. Queen Mary the Queen Mother also sent a letter of condolence; she had sent a small watercolour painting to Lynton in 1949 to raise money for local charities at the annual Christmas Fair. The British Government donated £25,000 and soon cheques, postal orders, and money was sent from all over the country to aid the victims. Cities, towns, and villages started a relief fund. London theatres held performances giving the proceeds to Lynmouth. Villagers at Burwash in Sussex collected £45; employees of M.G. & Riley Cars at Abingdon sent £62 and from the sale of a tractor and plough, David Brown Tractors donated the proceeds of £547.

Dunbar Town Council in Scotland sponsored a swimming gala arranged by Steve Mellors, the manager of the local swimming pool, their efforts raising £226. Many donations were from people, who in the past had stayed in Lynmouth on holiday, a postal order for £1 was sent just signed "a lover of Lynmouth" along with many others offering similar sentiments to the village.

Bowling clubs, scout troops, pubs and clubs, cinemas, people throughout the land generously supported the little Devon village that had been devastated. By Monday morning, over £30,000 had been raised and it wasn't long before world-wide donations started to arrive. The English Speaking Union of Boston, Massachusetts sent a cheque for £100. An office of the New Zealand Red Cross society sent £5 to the Town Hall.

At the end of the week £151,000 had been sent, an unbelievable amount of money in 1952. By the end of October the fund stood at over £1,250,000. When the fund was closed four years later in August 1956, a total of £1,336,425 had been contributed.

Lynton Town Hall received telegrams from building companies offering tiles, bricks, timber and roofing felt.

An American shipping line, Lykes Bros. of New Orleans, offered many items of clothing from the stores of their ship, the SS Louise Lykes, which at the time was docked at Liverpool. These were gratefully accepted by the Town Clerk, Leonard Ridge, on behalf of the village. HM Customs & Excise waived the customs duty on the jackets, shirts, dungarees and 12 pairs of underpants (Heavy duty).

## Other Areas Affected

Although the flood is always referred to as The Lynmouth Flood, it affected a much wider area of the region. By far the worst loss of life, damage to properties and devastation was in Lynmouth, but there were lives lost, suffering, hardship and serious damage to property throughout North Devon and West Somerset that day.

At Parracombe in the Heddon Valley five miles from Lynmouth, the culvert of an old disused railway embankment blocked causing water to build up behind. During the evening at about 9:30 pm,

*Parracombe circa 1910.*

*Parracombe after the flood.*

the River Heddon started to flow over the little stone bridge in the centre of the village. Customers in the Fox & Goose by the side of the river, jumped on top of the bar as the water entered the hotel rising rapidly. The level receded and every one went home excitedly. Showing concern, the village postman William Leaworthy (60) who lived at Rose Cottage, decided he would see how his sister-in-law, Miss Tamlyn of nearby South Hill Cottage was coping. He died at about 12-45am trying to scramble to safety when the embankment collapsed, causing a tidal wave of water to roar through the village. In the morning he was found a mile away at West Hill Farm. All people could do when they heard the deafening noise was to bolt their doors quickly. When the wave struck the cottages in the path of the torrent, the front and back doors simultaneously burst open under the pressure, allowing trees and debris to smash through the buildings.

On holiday from Woking, teacher Mrs. Alys Thorne (46) and her 14-year-old son Roger were asleep in a chalet at Mill Farm. The chalet disintegrated instantly when the wall of water enveloped it. Their bodies were found a mile down the valley next morning. Mrs. Thorne's husband Reginald had left Parracombe on Wednesday to watch their elder son play cricket at Lord's. He had been selected to play for the English Schools Eleven against the MCC young professionals. Returning to continue his holiday on Saturday morning, Mr. Thorne was told of the tragedy as he drove through the village to meet his wife and younger son.

Near South Molton just to the south of Exmoor, a troop of twenty-one Boy Scouts from Moss-side in Manchester were camping on Lord Fortescue's land at Shallowford. Having arrived two days before, the decision was to retire early on the Friday evening because of the wet conditions. At 12-30 am the River Bray overflowed and swamped the campsite nearby. Tents and equipment were washed away as most of the boys were making for safety at the nearest house. Rev.Wieland, the curate in charge and the Assistant Scoutmaster, rescued one scout who was clinging to the branch of a tree near the river. But three poor lads lost their lives. The police recovered the bodies of Harold Shaw (14), Derrick Breddy (11) and Geoffrey Robinson (11) next morning. For a year, young Derrick had saved his weekly pocket money of two shillings towards his first holiday with his friends. Local collections raised the money to replace the £400 worth of equipment that the scouts had lost. Residents in the area quickly gathered clothes and necessities needed by the troop and there was no shortage of local support for the frightened lads.

At Tarr Steps near Dulverton, the ancient clapper bridge was washed away by the River Barle except for one seven foot section. The bridge comprises of stones weighing up to 2 tons laid end to end on stone supports and is the longest clapper bridge in England, although its age is uncertain. One clapper stone of 1 ton had been carried 157 feet by the force of the water.

After the flood, all the missing stones were recovered downstream and the bridge rebuilt. More than once this historic river crossing has been washed away or damaged by flood but all stones are now numbered to facilitate rebuilding, which proved useful when Royal Engineers last rebuilt it in 1961 after flood damage.

Just below this ancient crossing is a flat 15-acre field adjoining the river. Next morning over 300 dead trout were seen lying mysteriously uninjured over the meadow where the flood had reached the previous night. A local angler was asked why the fish were not bruised by the battering floodwater. His explanation was that the rising waters had allowed the fish to exploit a fresh feeding ground. The flood had receded as quickly as it had risen and the overfed trout were left gasping and stranded.

*The Golden Guernsey Milk Bar, Dulverton.*

In nearby Winsford some houses were flooded to a height of four feet, including the cottage that Labour Minister Ernest Bevin was born in. Other homes had water up to the ceilings. Two bridges in the village suffered considerable damage.

Dulverton, the small town at the foot of Exmoor, was also a scene of destruction on the Saturday morning. The River Barle runs through the lower part of the town where luckily the damage was mostly confined to the area of the Town Bridge, away from the main residential area. The more conventional character of this south flowing Exmoor river, compared to the Lyn rivers, meant the damage was caused by the amount of water, rather than the combined force of water and boulders that reeked havoc in Lynmouth. Large trees dammed against the bridge causing the flow to divert either side, isolating the central part of the structure. Motor vehicles were washed down river when the overwhelming force badly damaged Batten & Thorne's garage. As the water diverted, it swept into a row of four buildings, causing damage beyond repair to Mr. Cleave's cottage and the popular Golden Cream dairy next door. Although many buildings were flooded to a considerable height causing damage, there was no loss of life as local police were able to evacuate residents just in time. Their warning had come from a village 'bobby' twelve miles away who had experienced the flood first hand.

Exford lies in a valley at the heart of the moor. In the early stage of its life, the River Exe normally flows through the village no more than a large stream. P.C. Hutchings received a call that a landslide was blocking the road near Simonsbath seven miles away. As he rode his motor cycle towards the village in the pouring rain to investigate, a wall of water suddenly threw him off his machine onto the road. Recovering, and realising the threat to his own village he remounted, but the bike would not respond to his efforts to start it. He coasted the machine down the long hill leading to the centre of Exford. Making his way to the White Horse Hotel, he found the water level already rising in the building. He just had time to make the crucial telephone call to his fellow officers at Dulverton before everybody in the hotel was forced to evacuate upstairs. Being at the centre of hunting country, the Hotel had a large stable at the rear. One of the grooms released over twenty horses who fled to higher ground. They were all rounded up a couple of days later, dishevelled, but none the worse for their ordeal.

At Brendon in the Oare Valley, the flooded East Lyn was causing havoc throughout the village. Mrs Kathleen Burge of Parsonage Farm was visiting her grandmother at Malmsmead Farm a couple of miles away when the baby she was expecting caused her to go into labour. Unable to return home because of the flooded roads, a call was made for an ambulance, which could not assist immediately due to flooded conditions in the area. An 8lb baby boy was born soon after with the help of grandmother and female relatives who were at hand. When the ambulance finally arrived, make-do stepping stones were used to carry them to the vehicle and on to Minehead Hospital where mother and child soon made a full recovery.

*Prince Philip, Duke of Edinburgh arrives in October 1952 - a welcome boost to the villagers' moral.*

*Mrs Dorothy Slater describes the devastation to Prince Philip with the aid of a picture postcard.*

## Housing

Housing the homeless people of Lynmouth was in the hands of Jack Pedder, Chairman of the local Housing Committee. Spare houses were not available and nearly a hundred dwellings were urgently needed. Local councils throughout the West Country were quick to respond to the disaster with offers of help. Bristol Councillors unanimously offered ten new council houses and eleven flats to those who had lost their homes. In conjunction with Lady Eldon, Deputy President of the Devon Red Cross, Mr. Pedder, who worked tirelessly throughout this period, issued an appeal to the country for caravans. He was quoted as saying, "It is better than pushing people into requisitioned houses where they may not be wanted or where families will be split up. People can name the caravans after their former homes - Sunnyside, Rose Cottage or Tor Bridge Cottage. They will not feel so uprooted and can continue to deal with local shops, the children can still go to a local school with their friends". Here was a man who had a true feeling of the villagers' troubles at heart. Manufacturers immediately donated fully equipped vans, private individuals from all over Britain, with guidance from the Caravan Club, sacrificed their own holidays and gave treasured vans on loan. Nationwide response was so great that at the end of a fortnight, over thirty caravans were ready for occupation. A site had quickly been prepared at Holman Park in Lynton, where the Hotpoint Company had kindly donated a fully equipped laundry. In all, fifty caravans were in use until March 1953 by which time every one had been re-housed. This park, at the entrance to the Valley of Rocks, is still used by villagers today as a recreation ground. Costain, the civil engineering Company presented the Council with a pair of houses that are still standing in Lee Road. Most families, who decided to stay, moved into a new estate of houses and bungalows that had been erected at the top of Lynton near the Valley of Rocks. Prince Philip, Duke of Edinburgh officially opened them in October 1952 whilst visiting Lynmouth to see the devastation that had been caused. These twenty-eight dwellings were refurbished in 2003 and continue to house members of the local community.

## Funeral

Friday afternoon on 22nd August was warm and sunny with a gentle breeze blowing through the Valley of Rocks. The cemetery, set on the lower southern slope of the hillside, was thronging with people attending the sombre occasion. All walks of life were represented as the long procession made its way to the resting place of thirteen local victims of the disaster. Villagers, members of the armed services and dignitaries dressed in their formal uniform of office walked alongside local fishermen wearing their familiar navy blue jumpers. Local firemen, who had acted with such valour during the tragedy, walked solemnly as they carried the coffins steadily to the gravesides. Six members of the Floyd family were laid to rest together, poignantly adding to the tragedy that had fallen on the village. The sobbing of families and friends broke the muffled sound of the nearby sea as Lynton vicar, the Rev. Soutter, conducted the service with the Vicar of Lynmouth the Rev. A.T. Coldman. As the solemn occasion ended, a lone piper from the Scots Fusiliers piped a final tribute to the men, women and children that had been so cruelly taken from the community.

A Memorial Service to those who had lost their lives was held a fortnight after the disaster at 3-30 pm on Friday the 29th August in St Mary's Church Lynton. As the tragedy had aroused the sympathy and concern of the country, the BBC attended to broadcast the service to the nation. Again both local vicars conducted the event.

Although St. John Baptist parish church in Lynmouth had suffered little damage during the flood, it was impossible to hold the service there. This was due to the condition of the village and the fact that it was still an exclusion zone to residents and the public. However, at the request of the many workers in the village, the Salvation Army held a small service at the same time in the centre of Lynmouth. After a fortnight of constant day and night noise and activity, the village fell silent for the first time. Only the voice of Brigadier Mrs. Holland could be heard as she conducted the short but moving service.

On October 22nd 1953, the Lord Bishop of Exeter dedicated an oak Memorial Vestry in the church. Members of the United States Air Force serving in Britain had generously contributed to it. In the past, many American tourists had fallen for the charms of Lynmouth forming an affinity that exists to this day.

On the vestry, a tablet lists all the victims who died in the disaster; most of those listed from Lynmouth had been members of the church congregation.

It was the first day of November 1952 before the villagers of Lynmouth had cause for happiness in their parish church. On that day, the first wedding since the disaster took place at St John Baptist

Church. Frances, daughter of Tom Slann who owned the Granville Hotel, was married to Frank Ramsbottom, an army officer. Lynmouth people celebrated the joyous occasion and the realisation that perhaps their village was going to recover from the wasted ruins that surrounded them. In what form nobody could imagine, but amongst them a quiet determination was growing. In fact, the normally slow wheels of authority had been turning since mid-August with regard to the permanent restitution of Lynmouth.

Twenty eight people lost their lives in or very near to Lynmouth. Three young scouts were swept away from their camp at Filliegh near South Molton. A local man and a holidaymaker with her son were lost at Parracombe. The following lists deaths that occurred in the North Devon & West Somerset Flood of August 15th 1952:

*Friday August 22 1952.*

| Name | Age | Address |
|---|---|---|
| Ronald Bowen | 37 | Lynton |
| Elsie D. Bowen | 32 | Lynton |
| David T. Bowen | 11 | Lynton (Missing, believed drowned) |
| Kenneth R. F. Bowen | 9 | Lynton |
| Mary A. Floyd | 64 | Lynton |
| Frederick C. Floyd | 27 | Lynton |
| William N. Richards | 30 | Lynmouth |
| Gwendoline A. Richards | 32 | Lynmouth |
| Bernard G. Richards | 3 | Lynmouth |
| Ernest W. Richards | 3 months | Lynmouth |
| Gabriel J. Litson | 78 | Lynmouth |
| Charles H. Litson | 53 | Lynmouth |
| Maud E. Watts | 72 | Lynmouth |
| William H. Watts | 80 | Lynmouth |
| Benjamin Coult | 56 | Langley Park, Co Durham |
| Emma Coult | 52 | Langley Park, Co Durham |
| Alys Thorne | 46 | Westfield, Woking, Surrey |
| Roger Thorne | 14 | Westfield, Woking, Surrey |
| Elizabeth Cannon | 75 | Lynmouth (Missing, believed drowned) |
| Hannah Jarvis | 77 | Lynmouth |
| Emily Ridd | 54 | Lynton |
| Rodney G. Dimmock | 8 | Lynton |
| Ada Barwick | 60 | Lynmouth |
| Stella Bates | 40 | Bedford (Missing, believed drowned) |
| Derek Breddy | 11 | Moss-side, Manchester |
| Elsie Cherry | 56 | Highgate, London |
| Joyce Hiscock | 21 | Melbourne, Australia |
| William J. Leaworthy | 60 | Parracombe |
| Gwenda Oxley | 22 | Melbourne, Australia |
| Geoffrey Robinson | 11 | Moss-side, Manchester |
| Harold Shaw | 14 | Chorlton-on-Medlock, Manchester |
| Edwin Smith | 50 | Lynmouth |
| Jessie Whitbread | 48 | Bedford (Missing, believed drowned) |
| One lady unidentified | | |

## Highest Rainfall

It should be remembered that for 24 hours it rained heavily on Lynmouth before and during the village's ordeal. Frequently the downpour was torrential during this period. The 9.1 inches (230 mm) that fell in 24 hours at the time of the Lynmouth flood is often quoted as the highest rainfall ever recorded in Britain. This is not so, on 25th June 1917, 9.56 inches (243 mm) of rain fell in 24 hours at Bruton in Mid Somerset. At the time, the worst ever recorded in the British Isles. In August 1924, 9.4 inches (232 mm) of rain fell in 24 hours at Cannington in West Somerset. In both these areas, the landscape is flatter than Exmoor and floodwater levels were lower having a wider area to disperse. The rain fell consistently over the 24 hours on both these events, not with extreme periods of rainfall during that time. Three cases of rainfall exceeding 9 inches in a span of 35 years are not classed as infrequent. Although all were coincidentally in the West Country, none of the rainfalls were in the same catchment area.

During 1952 there was a high incidence of heavy thunderstorms in the South West and West Midlands areas of Britain for a four month period starting from April. Extreme storms had occurred on 16th April, 19th May, 13th June, and 1st and 6th July. Exmoor had been badly affected by the thunderstorm on 16th April that year. The small depression culminating in the great storm that created the flood of 1952, developed over the North Atlantic and was first apparent to the Meteorological Office on 12th August moving east-southeast. On the 15th August between 3 and 6 pm the centre of the depression had moved north to near Exeter. A warm front had moved up from France causing thunderstorms in the English Channel, but the main outbreak of rain reached Plymouth just before 7 am drifting slowly north and was over North Devon and the Bristol Channel area at about 3 pm.

Over the catchment area of the Lyn rivers, the rainfall during the 24 hours was extraordinary. The greatest intensity was measured at the headwaters of the West Lyn River at Hoaroak Water and Farley Water. From the area of Pinkworthy near Challacombe, it was estimated that at times 6-8 inches of water was flowing over the high ground of the moor. There seems no doubt that this level of flow was happening on many parts of Exmoor. Over the period, 9.1 inches (230 mm) of rain was measured on the gauge at Longstone Barrow sited on the west of the moor. Out of this total, 7 inches (178 mm) fell in seven hours and 6 inches (153 mm) in five hours. This rain gauge had been set up by the Meteorological Office only a year previously in August 1951, and was the only official gauge in the area of heaviest rainfall that day. Due to its remote position 1550 feet up on the moor, it was read monthly, but luckily the voluntary observer, Mr. C.H. Archer, had taken the initiative to read the gauge on 14th and 16th August. Although this meter has been quoted as the only official gauge in the area, another was in use at the time. Readings from a gauge sited at Lillycombe cottage near Culbone in West Somerset showed a level of 4.5 inches of rain over the 24 hour period.

Other clues to help give a better picture of the downfall came to light. By chance, a pressure cooker and a bucket had been left out at Brendon Barton campsite in the East Lyn valley. Five inches of rain were measured in these unorthodox "rain-gauges". An amount of 4 inches was found in a well-sheltered old bucket at Furzehill near Barbrook.

One of the most interesting measurements that came to light was at Simonsbath where a cylindrical bucket left in the middle of a field was found to contain 10 inches of water. Loss of water because of splashing may have meant a level of over 11 inches of rain in 24 hours, but if that were so, the heavy fall would have been very local.

The thin layer of topsoil and heather covering the moors and valleys was saturated already and could not absorb any more of the constant deluge. Underneath was the impervious rock of Exmoor, the result was an enormous flow of water streaming into the headwaters of the Lyn rivers and carving fresh deep ravines into the landscape. Water appeared suddenly from valley sides creating the local legend that the moors had burst. The torrent created exceeded the official British level of *Acute Catastrophic Flood*. Consequent assessment of the event decided that it should be included on the list of *Extreme Flood Discharges of the World*. The river Lyn's comparatively small catchment area of 39 square miles produced an amount of water that has only twice been exceeded by the 3,812 square mile catchment area of the Thames since records of that river began in 1883.

It has been calculated that 900 tons of rain per acre fell on the drainage area of the Lyn rivers that day, enough to supply Lynmouth for 108 years.As the flood waters tore down the narrow valley sweeping all before them, mature trees were wrenched from the soil. Ten, twenty, thirty, even forty-ton boulders were swept along the river, some demolishing buildings that lay in their path. A 63-ton boulder, estimated to have travelled at least half a mile, was removed from the harbour during rebuilding of the village. In all, over 6000 cu. yards of rock were deposited around the village that day equating to 15,000 tons of boulders, mostly from the West Lyn river. The estimated total of debris that was removed after the flood from the streets and rivers of Lynmouth was 114,000 tons. That amount was rammed into an area only three-quarters of a mile long by an average three hundred yards wide.

Shortly after the disaster it was queried whether a burst dam had caused the flood. At Woolhanger, 3 miles south of Lynmouth, there was a reservoir on the main tributary flowing into the West Lyn at Barbrook. When the excessive rainfall caused the 30-feet retaining wall of Southdown Lake to breach, it quickly released its 1,500,000 gallons of water into the river. It is known that the dam burst at approximately 9:10 pm. The four cottages swept away by the West Lyn at Barbrook with the loss of twelve lives, happened at about 9:30 pm. In fact, the burst dam did not cause the flood but the onrush of water added to the already overflowing river and would appear to have contributed to the loss of life that night.

Generally, we think of flooding in Britain as damage caused mainly by just the height of water. The Lynmouth flood was caused by a combination of extreme rainfall, the fact that there was no flood storage due to the narrow Lyn Valleys, and the unusually steep gradient of the rivers causing the dynamic effect of the torrent, coupled with its load of boulders and debris. What also compounded the tragedy was the position of properties built on sites that would be vulnerable during extreme flooding. This human mistake had unwittingly happened as the village expanded. Another contributing factor was that the valley sides were private property and little maintenance was carried out. Consequently, large trees that were growing or had fallen near the riverbed, were swept away helping to block river bridges. Surge waves 30 feet high swept down on the village as the dams that had formed gave way under the immense pressure behind them. These large surges moved material that otherwise would have remained in place.

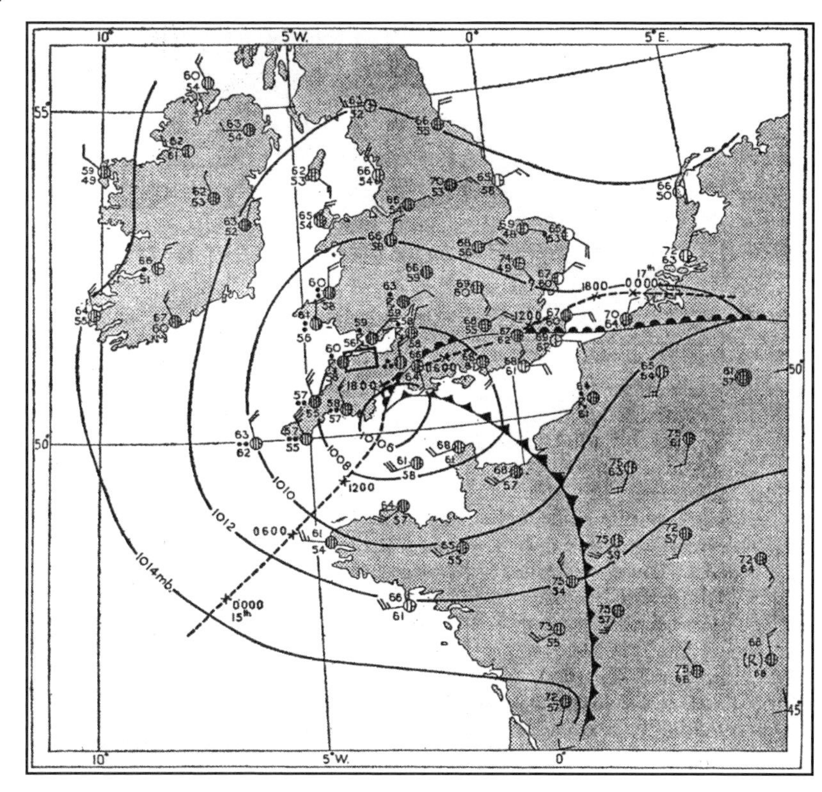


*Weather map for 15th August 1952. The small rectangle covers Exmoor (shown opposite).*

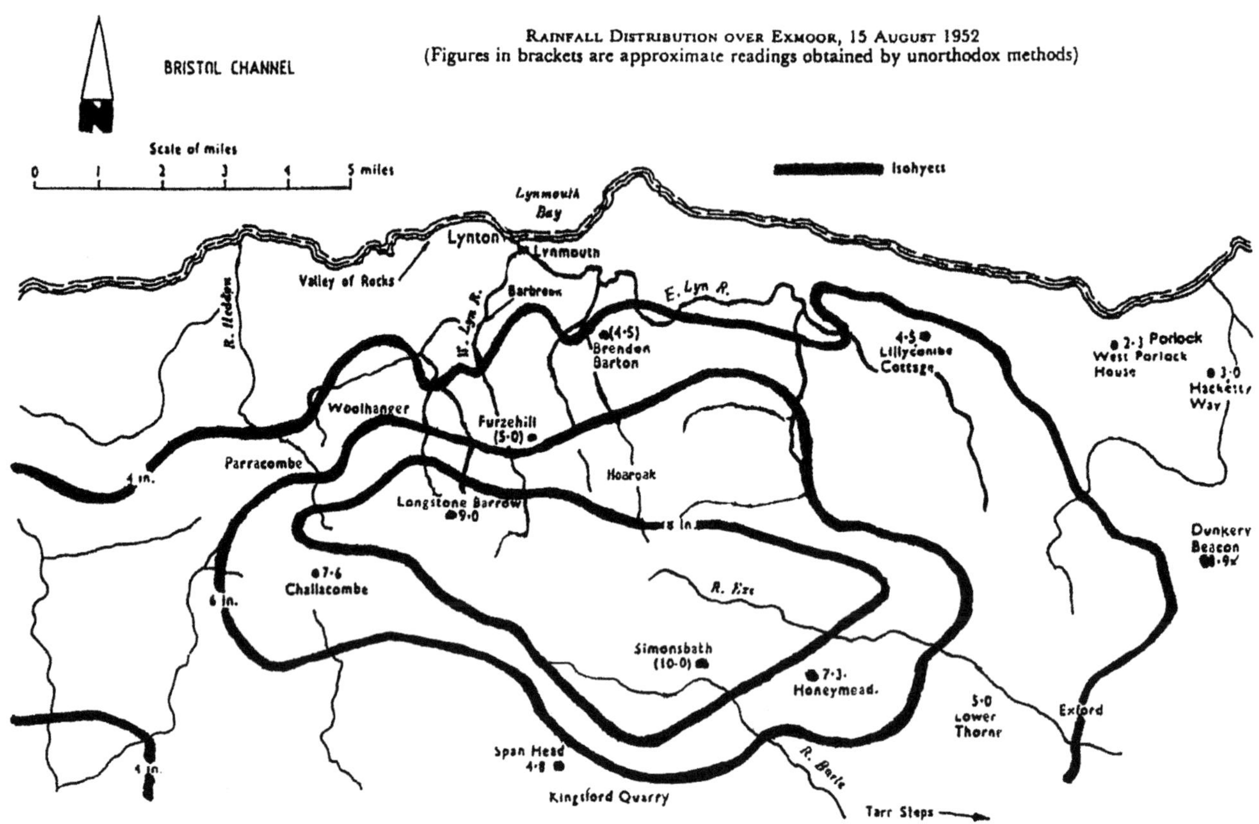


*Plan of rivers with isohyet contours (based on Fig. 9 Dobbie & Wolf 1953 modified).*

## Flood Levels

The flood levels in Lynmouth on the night of 15th August were clearly seen the next day. All over the village the muddy watermarks were apparent on wrecked and surviving buildings (opposite). Missing doors and smashed windows lower down gave way to the usual appearance of the upper level where the water had not risen. Some buildings were damaged to the eaves, showing where the flooding had reached to the roof. Along the East and West Lyn valleys, the level reached by the water was obvious, where trees and foliage had previously skirted the river edge, bare banks rose up over 30 feet (9.2 m) in places. Today, a marker on the face of the Glen Lyn Gorge is sited over 50 feet from the normal level of the West Lyn.

When considering the various flood levels reached in the village, it must be remembered that the wide expanse of boulders and debris were up to 25 feet deep in parts and became a temporary riverbed. The positions of the following list of actual levels can be seen on the picture of the village shown on page 67.

| Building | Height above Normal River level.(feet) |
|---|---|
| Bath Hotel. | 21.1 |
| Lyn Valley Hotel. | 32.2 |
| West Lyn Cafe. | 37.5 |
| Granville Hotel. | 46.1 |
| The Falls. | 47.8 |
| Lyndale Hotel. | 55.5 |
| Lyndale Hotel. | 60.0 (East Lyn side of hotel) |

During maximum surge of the West Lyn, the water travelling down the 600 yd stretch from the Glen Lyn gorge to the village had to dissipate energy at the rate of 350,000 horse power as it flowed at 40 feet/ second (12.3metres / sec).

The picture below is a photograph of a model of Lynmouth before the flood. The relative proximity and the level of the flood water recorded at the different hotels is shown.

| Lyn Valley Hotel | West Lyn Cafe | Falls Hotel | Granville Hotel | Lyndale Hotel | Lyndale Hotel (east) |
|---|---|---|---|---|---|
| 32.2ft | 37.5ft | 47.8ft | 46.1ft | 55.5ft | 60ft |

## River Flow & Levels.

After the flood it was difficult to measure the amount of water that had flowed through the village that night. Devon River Board had been formed in 1950 and was responsible for the two rivers. However, at the time of the disaster, the Board had not yet delegated the East and West Lyn waters. In those days, there was not an emphasis on the management of rivers as practiced today. For instance, widespread use of nitrates and chemicals that can contaminate watercourses was not as prevalent in those days as its use is today. Fallen trees that could restrict river flows were not always removed, they were looked upon as picturesque once lichen and moss had covered them, even serving as convenient crossing points. In fact, during a severe gale in March 1952, four large trees had fallen in the Glen Lyn Gorge near the West Lyn, undoubtedly adding to the debris that blocked the narrow channel causing the river to divert. No gauging stations had been installed to record the various flows and depths along the course of each river.

In conjunction with the Ministry of Agriculture and Fisheries, the Devon River Board decided to commission a report on the event. They engaged a respected civil engineer, Mr. Charles H Dobbie, BSc. M.I.C.E. F.G.S. M.I.W.E., of Victoria St, London as their consultant.

Considering the difficulties, even for this competent engineer, credit must be given to him and his team for having the report ready within four months. Most of the time Mr. Dobbie's team took compiling the report was spent assessing the flows in the rivers during the flood. With no gauging stations, one rain gauge, and obviously no observer present, confirmed data of the flood was very limited, an assessment had to be inferred. A total of thirteen sites were selected along the two rivers where the flood water line was obvious by wrack marks. These levels may not, of course, have been a true water line, but the height of a surge after a temporary blockage upstream. It was reasonable to assume that where levels showed signs of scouring on the banks, there had been a longer period of flow. Surges would not leave time for scouring.

To help confirm calculations of the flow, the team found an unusual feature on the West Lyn. As the river passes through the Glen Lyn Gorge, a rocky cleft projects into the valley causing the river to travel in quick succession through a right-angled zigzag. As a point of interest, the small private hydroelectric power station of today built by Mr. Ken Oxenham, extracts its water supply from this point. At this narrow part of the gorge, the riverbed and sides are of solid rock and consequentially did not alter during the flood, making it an ideal site for research.

It was decided to make a 1/48-scale model of this section of the river so that by simulation, the flood levels could be confirmed by passing water through at different rates. This would also verify the volume of water that had passed through the West Lyn at the height of the flood.

A model was built of wax and wood for study in the Hawksley Hydraulic Laboratory at Imperial College, University of London. It was eventually found that a volume of water exceeding 500,000 gallons a day through the model confirmed calculations made on surveys carried out on site. This figure equates to an actual flow through the West Lyn river of a maximum 8,500 cusecs (cubic feet of water a second). When this flow is added to the longer East Lyn river, it shows that the volume of water travelling through the lower end of the village that night, was at times, totalling 23,000 cusecs, or approximately 651 cubic metres a second. Normally after rainfall, the flow of water travelling into the sea is approximately 8 cubic metres a second. Why so much time and effort was taken to determine the flow figures was because these would determine the new channel sizes and so form the basis for rebuilding the village.

Another consideration would be the tidal range of the Bristol Channel that the Lyn rivers flow into. In places around its coast, the tidal range of the Channel is amongst the highest in the world. At Lynmouth a neap tide is 15 feet (4.6m), a spring tide can draw over 29 feet (8.9m). The height of a tide would have a bearing on the river flow through the village during a time of flood. Floodwater meeting the obstruction of an exceptionally high tide, would cause levels to rise throughout the village.

With all facts taken into account, Mr. Dobbie's report recommended the following flow figures as a basis for the redesign of a safe Lynmouth.

| River | Catchment area Acres | Design flow Cusecs | Peak flow Cusecs |
|---|---|---|---|
| East Lyn. | 19,240 | 20,000 | 22,000 |
| West Lyn. | 5,720 | 10,000 | 12,000 |
| Lyn. | 24,960. | 25,000 | 30,000 |

As far as the 1952 flood is concerned, it could be said that sadly, Lynmouth was a victim of its own success. Demand for buildings started from the time that the village first attracted visitors early in the 19th century. It is not uncommon for buildings to be erected on the flood plain of a river, accepting through history the rare occasion of flooding.

Lynmouth was built on the bed of an immature river, the consequences of which were only realised after the flood. In mitigation, history showed that flooding on this scale only occurred every few hundred years or so. Ideally, the rebuilding of Lynmouth would be based on its history of recurring flooding over a long period, but no river gauging records existed. Development space was limited as the village grew to the demands the increase in tourism put upon it. Understandably, local people may well have treated the 1769 flood as an isolated event as they expanded the village.

The mistake of building on potentially unsafe sites in Lynmouth was a very human one, but no one person or authority can be blamed for the devastation caused by the 1952 event. Before the flood, the harbour at Lynmouth was important to the commerce of the village in as much as its use for leisure, fishing, pleasure cruises and the embarking and disembarking of the many visitors that came on the large paddle steamers calling during the summer months.

*Rhenish Tower August 1954.*

Villagers were anxious that these activities should return in time for the following 1953 season. The restitution of the harbour arm, which protected the haven and had been destroyed, was paramount, considering that during the winter of 1952/53, scouring of the west beach from the sea was apparent due to the loss of the arm. Because of the urgency, and the fact that it would not affect the final plan of the village, construction of the arm was commenced early in 1953. A small causeway was added which would give better protection to the west beach. A replica Rhenish Tower in the original position was incorporated due too its previous importance as the focal point of the harbour and because of the old tower's historic value to Lynmouth. Lynton Urban District Council and the community requested an exact replica of the tower, which posed a problem as no records or plans existed of the old structure. An interesting fact is that Blackford, the main contractor, rebuilt the tower entirely with the help of old picture postcards. Following the flood, the wrought iron beacon that had stood on top of the tower was found amidst wreckage on the foreshore. Although damaged, it was repaired and refitted to the new tower in August 1954. Originally, a wood fire in the basket guided vessels to the harbour at night or when conditions were foggy. Today, a red light switched on at dusk lends authenticity to the well-known landmark.

Estimated costs for rebuilding the Harbour and Sea Defenses were:

| | |
|---|---|
| Harbour. dredging | £12,500 |
| Harbour arm & apron | £25,500 |
| Groyne & causeway | £11,500 |
| For temporary harbour | £25,500 |
| Total | £75,000 |

Urgent Sea Defence works in readiness for 1953 season:

| | |
|---|---|
| Apron to sea wall | £6,500 |
| Groynes & Western end of Esplanade | £34,000 |

(All costs are at 1953 value)

Suggestions were made for building a deep-water harbour to enable steamers to berth at Lynmouth quayside. It was soon realised that the idea was not practical as the harbour size would be reduced due to a new river training arm. Also the shallow depth of the rocky approach to the harbour from the sea.

*Foundations of the river training arm.*

## Rebuilding

There were reasons peculiar to the village that had to be considered when planning the rebuilding programme. Since the late 18th century Lynmouth had relied on its unique romantic character and appearance to attract the visitor. Beside the deep wooded valleys and impressive sea cliffs, the array of individual 19th century buildings were an integral part of the village's character and completed the picture loved by so many. The welcome that visitors still receive is an extension of the pride that locals have always had of their villages. Lynton and Lynmouth compliment each other and are truly 'twin resorts'. Even today, there are very few who having visited the area once, fail to visit again. The consultant engineer's report on the recommended plan to rebuild Lynmouth was submitted to Devon River Board and Devon County Council by mid-November 1952. Copies were circulated to all relevant parties including, of course, Lynton & Lynmouth Urban District Council. Publishing the report so promptly showed the commitment Mr. Dobbie and his team had given to this consultation.

*Riverside Road replaces the Lyn river which has been moved and widened. The flood plain is on the left.*

Rebuilding Lynmouth was going to be a major undertaking. Whatever the civil engineering work that had to be carried out, those deciding the design would have to make extremely difficult and bold decisions. The main bodies involved in considering the various plans and implementing the final design, were Devon County Council, Devon River Board and the Lynton Urban District Council, who probably had the hardest decisions to make owing to their intimacy with the village. Devon County Surveyor Mr.R.B.Carnegie and Mr. Dobbie also attended the first of many meetings, helping to guide with their professional experience, along with a number of technical officers from interested Government Ministries. Coincidentally, Mr. Carnegie was also

Chief Engineer to the Devon River Board, which helped co-ordination between the two authorities. On the one hand, safety of residents and visitors was paramount but on the other hand, the village could not afford to lose its unique identity. There were three approaches to the rebuilding; firstly, a design that would make the village safe if a storm of this magnitude fell in the area again. This approach would restore public confidence and encourage people and their families to live and visitors to stay in the resort. Secondly, and the cheapest alternative at £120,000, would be to rebuild the harbour wall much as it was, pitch most of the river banks, tidy up and leave Lynmouth in its natural condition. Buildings would be demolished that were in a vulnerable position if a flood occurred again. Bridges would be replaced and escape routes provided throughout the village to prevent loss of life. A plan of this nature would not encourage residential visitors and would only attract day-trippers. Local people could not be blamed for initially favouring this plan as pride and love for the village they knew overcame any practical reason to rebuild to a safer design. Quietly a realisation that Lynmouth as they knew it could never return was reluctantly accepted.

*September 1954. Lynmouth Harbour takes shape.*

The third approach was to provide the greatest possible safety measures, paying no regard to the ultimate cost when related to the value of the properties to be protected. This plan was rejected not only on the grounds of cost, but because it involved wide rivers, dams and flood channels that would transform and ruin the character of the village. The second approach brought very little support. A huge response from Britain and the world, not only to the victims, but showing the special affection held for the village could not be ignored. Warning systems could not be guaranteed and it was important that the new design should impart confidence in the minds of all that lived in, and visited the village.

After many long meetings and discussions with interested parties, one of the three proposals was agreed upon in principle. It was a culmination of ideas and considerations from all that were involved in the rebuilding plan including, of course, the local residents. On 12th February 1953, a public meeting was held in Lynton Town Hall when residents and the Town Council gave overwhelming support to the first scheme. This was outlined as: to take all precautions suggested in the Dobbie report and at the same time use the opportunity presented to improve the road system of Lynmouth. At a Devon County planning meeting in late February 1953, this scheme was adopted as the plan for the rebuilding of Lynmouth. One point agreed by all parties was that major civil engineering work should be carried out during winter months. This would mean that rebuilding would take four years to complete, but the village needed to re-establish commerce quickly, and would need the influx of summer visitors to be unhindered by workings.

*The new Lyndale Bridge.*

Mr and Mrs Aubrey Braunton who kept the Bath Hotel noticed a typical effect on trade during the late autumn of 1953. Pile drivers had to work on the harbour defenses according to the tide. When the slumber of one guest was disturbed at 2 o'clock in the morning, he hastily booked out of the hotel early next day.

National and worldwide coverage of the disaster coupled with natural curiosity meant that many people would be visiting Lynmouth in the foreseeable future.

Of all the many practical, soul-searching and emotional decisions to make by all concerned with the rebuilding of Lynmouth, one issue caused more argument than any other.

The bone of contention was over the three replacement bridges to be built in the village. Lynton Urban District Council wanted all the road bridges to be of a stone arch design as this type of bridge is "traditional to Lynmouth and its environment". They pointed out, quite rightly, that there was no engineering reason why a stone design could not be built. There was no objection by Mr. Carnegie with regard to the wider Lyndale Bridge, but the two bridges crossing the West Lyn at Prospect Corner and Lynmouth Street would have to be modern pre-stressed concrete structures incorporating reinforced steel joists because of the limited headroom. The council replied that a concrete design "..would injure amenity and would be found offensive by the local people and indeed by the people of the country at large." Devon C.C. Highways Department was insistent on the new design of bridge, saying that the difference of bank heights would not be suitable for a stone structure. As far as they were concerned, an unsightly hump would be introduced with a stone bridge and extra expense would be needed to raise the riverbanks. The heated argument over the bridge design continued until March 1957 when the Ministry of Housing & Local Government informed the Lynton Town Clerk that a concrete slab bridge was to be the final approved design. Lynton Council had fought hard but eventually with great reluctance, they had to admit defeat, accepting the small consolation that this was the first time the new technique of pre-stressed concrete was to be used to build a Devon bridge. Even today the two river crossings are looked upon by locals and visitors as an eyesore and out of character with Lynmouth.

The cost of building the new Lynmouth bridges was:

| Bridge | Old arch span | New span | Cost |
|---|---|---|---|
| Lyndale Bridge (A39) | 30ft | 80 feet | £37,000 |
| Lynmouth Street | 12ft | 83 feet 5in | £30,659 |
| Prospect Corner | 15ft | 51 feet 3in | £28,000 |

From these figures it would appear that the insistence by higher authorities for installing concrete bridges across the West Lyn was purely cost.

In 1956, the ruins of Sir George Newnes mansion, Hollerday House, became unsafe. Now owned by the local council, it was demolished in September that year. A foot bridge that had been washed away at Lynbridge on the West Lyn, had been replaced with a temporary wooden structure soon after the flood. Devon County Council decided to reinstate the stone bridge on the site in 1957. Stone from Hollerday House was used to build the new bridge thus continuing the great benefactors service to the community long after his death.

In his report, Mr. Dobbie had recommended four basic points that he felt were necessary to create a safe village:

1. Adequate channels and bridges should be constructed.
2. No buildings should be allowed on the area between the East and West Lyn rivers, and existing remains should be removed.
3. A relief channel should be constructed on the right bank across the recreation grounds in front of the Manor House.
4. Check dams to collect boulders should be constructed in both the East Lyn and West Lyn valleys.

Both point (1) and (2) were to be implemented in the plan, but point (3) would cut a swathe across the only large flat area in the village. This relief channel would be 220 feet wide running from the east beach to the Lyn river with shallow banks that would be grassed to impress on visitors that it was there for safety reasons alone. To reassure and emphasise this point, a putting green and tennis court could be incorporated in the channel replacing the facilities that already existed on the Manor green. At each end would be large concrete gates, opened primarily if ever the West Lyn flooded. Thankfully this idea was not accepted and a compromise was to build a flood plain by widening the Lyn river along the length of the Manor grounds to the harbour and open sea. This would allow for the extra volume of water from the West Lyn where it joins the East Lyn.

The Dobbie report thought the implementation of check dams to control the movement of boulders was "absolutely necessary" to the future safety of the village. Concrete dams faced with local stone would be built at inaccessible but strategic points on both rivers. Roads would have to be built to construct them and also serve as access for future maintenance of the structures. Creating impressive waterfalls 25 feet high, they could also help the village by serving as a local visitor attraction. This idea was rejected on grounds of cost and for aesthetic reasons. It was also felt that the planned increase in width of the rivers and bridges should cope adequately with moving boulders and debris in time of flood. The County Surveyor Mr. Carnegie pointed out that any accumulation of boulders due to a major flood in the future, would be in the Lynmouth river channels area. Here they could be dealt with easily because there would in future be better access to the riverside.

He also showed concern saying that the dams causing an increase in river height would interfere with the stability of the West Lyn valley sides. He may well have had a point, as three months after the flood an extensive landslide occurred on the valley road from Lynbridge to Lynmouth, luckily without injury to people or property. To widen the road it was necessary to cut into the rock face and excavate 12,000 tons of rock. Without a doubt, extreme scouring of the valley side during the flood had caused this slip.

Mr. W. N. McClean, a respected water engineer, suggested that escape tunnels for excessive floodwater might be built. Storage reservoirs on the East Lyn would be sited at Myrtleberry near Watersmeet and at Malmsmead in the Oare valley. These reservoirs would be connected to the sea by a mile long tunnel through the hillside. It was an idea that was discarded mainly on grounds of cost.

*Clearing the harbour.*

All 28 foot and road bridges on the rivers had been swept away or were damaged beyond repair. New footbridges would be of a 'weak' design. Instead of trees and debris blocking and damming a bridge, an extreme flood would cause the new structures to lift off the bearers and float away. Stone road bridges would have sufficient height and width to allow debris to pass and would be the same width as the proposed increased channel size of the rivers throughout the village. With a narrow channel, the velocity of the river flow would obviously be higher than that of a wider one. This was seen by the boulders that were swept down by the flood along the restricted width of the old river. But a channel too wide in Lynmouth would not be suitable for two reasons. Aesthetically it would ruin the appearance of the village as a large channel would be to wide for a narrow valley. Secondly, when river flow was normal it would be out of proportion to the width of the river. Vertical walls were to replace sloping banks thus keeping the width of rivers to a required minimum. It was recommended that the East Lyn, above its junction with the West Lyn, should be 80 feet (24.6m) wide and the West Lyn, 50 feet (15.4 m) wide from the end of the Glen Lyn Gorge.

*Widening the West Lyn (centre) meant the demolition of familiar hotels.*

From the junction to the sea, the Lyn would be 102 feet (31.4m) wide including the flood plain that would cater for extra water from the West Lyn if needed. All of the new river walls, including the harbour, were built of mass concrete reinforced with steel sheet piles to prevent scouring. The walls were faced with local flat stone laid on end (known locally as 'ditching') so as to drain water quickly. Some of the stone used had been recovered from the debris and wrecked buildings left by the flood.

To compensate for the desired width of channels recommended, throughout the village, the riverbed was deepened by 10 feet (3m). Previous to the flood, the average width of the East Lyn was only 35 feet . The boulder-strewn bed of the river was to be stabilised but retained so as to impede water velocity. A smooth riverbed would increase water velocity and ensure easier movement of boulders.

Widening the East and West Lyn would mean the loss of sites where established buildings had stood. Buildings such as the Lyn Valley Hotel, Granville Hotel, Falls Hotel, West Lyn Hotel, which dated from the mid to late 19th century were an integral part of Lynmouth and its history. But it remained essential that all buildings near the junction of the rivers were demolished and that no new structures were erected in this vulnerable area. Widening the Lyn rivers where they met would mean demolishing some of them anyway. It was suggested that the site of the Lyndale Hotel should be used as a water garden or car park. Because of the post-war increase of motor cars visiting during summer months, the area eventually became a car park and so it remains.

Lynmouth Street is a narrow road with buildings either side and no room to widen. Being the only thoroughfare to the harbour and Esplanade car park, it frequently created a bottleneck during the season. This problem was solved by creating a new road at the back of the block of buildings on the east side of Lynmouth Street. As the Lyn River was to be widened in any case, Riverside Road was to be built on the bed of the old river course serving two purposes. First to ease traffic through Lynmouth Street, and secondly, to act as a flood barrier for the lower end of the village. Looking at the buildings in Riverside Road today, it is difficult to imagine visitors fishing from the balconies as they once used to do.

Middleham, where the row of ten cottages had stood at the head of the village on the East Lyn, was never under consideration for rebuilding. The homes had been sited on the inside of a bend and in direct line of the river. On the night, the waters had demolished the buildings and scoured their foundations to the bedrock of the river, a depth of about 10 feet (3m). To rebuild on this site would be folly. Middleham is best left as it is with the surviving gardens of the cottages divided into plots of one square foot. Each plot has been sold in trust to a different person, ensuring the gardens remain as a memorial, never to be exploited. An adjoining plot of land is protected by a local Community Trust.

Out of 212 properties in Lynmouth, 52 were lost due to the flood. Some were swept completely away, not even the foundations showing afterwards, 12 were damaged beyond repair and pulled down. Sites of some of these buildings were lost to the river-widening scheme carried out through the village after the flood. Nearby, Barbrook lost four properties, although five families lost their homes.

It should be noted that some buildings housed apartments and a few hotels had staff quarters, therefore, a number of these buildings were home to more than one person or family. Over twenty properties had gardens in part or completely swept away besides the loss of garages and out-buildings.

There is no doubt that Lynmouth still has unique attributes that set it apart from any village in Britain. If Lynmouth had been rebuilt replacing some of the lost buildings, it would now possibly be a village of Victorian mixed with early post-war architecture. An indication of what may have prevailed is seen in the style of the two concrete bridges built over the West Lyn.

Since 1952, only six buildings have been erected in the village on previous sites. Opposite the harbour, the Flood Memorial Hall was erected in 1958 where the Lifeboat House had stood. Two shops were built on the site of the Lyn Valley Hotel next to the post office, as was a restaurant, which faces the West Lyn river. On Watersmeet Road, four retail units have taken the place of a garage, but these were a commercial arrangement erected in the 1980s and not in consequence of flood damage. Most of these buildings interrupt the original Victorian architecture surrounding them, just as a preserved older structure stands rudely surrounded by a monopoly of modem buildings in most towns of Britain today. The exception to these additional buildings in Lynmouth is the Flood Memorial Hall, which was constructed of local stone and sits comfortably in its surroundings.

A seventh building to be erected was a Plymouth Brethren Chapel built to replace the one lost that night. Also constructed of local stone it now serves as a water exhibition at the entrance to the Glen

Lyn Gorge. Standing near to the original site, this building was reconstructed in the character of late 19th century architecture.

Until the flood, Lynmouth was a village independent of Lynton as far as everyday trade was concerned. Its population was enough to support a butcher, grocer, greengrocer, chemist, shoe repairer, four garages, fruit shop, and a post office, beside the cafes, restaurants, and souvenir shops catering for holiday makers. Since 1952 with the necessary loss of so many homes and buildings that were never replaced, the population has shrunk to just over 100 people; the forced demise of the community was perhaps the saddest consequence of the disaster. This diminished number of residents are not sufficient to support service shops, especially in the winter months, although the post office still survives, retaining the George VI post-box that stood outside before the flood. Holiday homes that are only infrequently inhabited and even less in winter only compound the problem.

It could be supposed that today with the convenience and popular ownership of the motor car, the original service shops in Lynmouth might not still be trading as they did before the flood. Nowadays the permanent residents of Lynmouth communicate between the two villages more often than was once the case when few owned a motor vehicle. Perhaps the village may well have had to change anyway to manage with the increasing demand of the motor car. We shall never know. Service shops in Lynton now cope adequately for residents and visitors in the two villages, while both resorts cater equally with their range of shops for the visitor.

Holidays have changed over the years, generally the days are gone when your break from work took you to a British resort for a fortnight. Each summer brings a new sunny destination abroad that has become the popular place to visit. People can now afford to go to the exotic or adventurous places that are offered to them, perhaps even travelling halfway around the world. It is a sign of the ever-changing fashion of the British holidaymaker. Beside the day-tripper, Lynmouth and Lynton still attract visitors that stay for a week or more; the gentle pace, even in the height of summer counteracts the pressures of work and life that people experience in towns and cities. Increasingly the trend is for people to take short breaks throughout the year, for which the twin resorts cater perfectly.

Concern for the village had created an overwhelming response both national and internationally in 1952, putting those responsible for the rebuilding under an extreme obligation. Their foresight is to be commended considering the ignorance they had of how the future British holiday would be taken. Other than the two concrete bridges, the ultimate design decided upon was the best compromise available at the time. This is proven by the impression Lynmouth makes on visitors today. It is exactly the same impression as made on the visitors of yesteryear that helped create its legend. The rebuilding of the village was a success, for the essence of Lynmouth has survived.

## River Reclaiming Old Course

In the early spring of 1952, it was noticed that dippers frequenting the Watersmeet Valley were building their nests much higher in the banks of the East Lyn. Because of the birds' strange behaviour, some locals considered it a sign that the river levels would be higher that year. Perhaps nature was indeed warning of the impending disaster. George Richards, an elder of the village, had prophesied that one day the original course of the West Lyn would be reclaimed due to its interruption by the expansion of the village. In one particular case, buildings erected during the growth of the resort in the 19th century had encroached on the river (Lyn Valley Hotel and West Lyn Hotel and Cafe) restricting it to a narrow channel (opposite). By affecting the flow of the West Lyn, inevitably one day it would overflow and reclaim the bed of its original delta. In fact, during the 18th century the Lyn river flowed where Lynmouth Street runs today, until the road was built through the village in 1828. From the early 19th century until 1952, this group of buildings was known as the 'Island'. Lynmouth Bridge Restaurant on the east side of the street was called Island Cottage up to the time of the flood. But it should be understood that no river has a 'natural course'. Immature rivers like the East and West Lyn will alter their course depending on changing events such as, scouring of the banks, landslides, erosion, and the fall of large boulders. On rare occasions, sections of Watersmeet Road in the East Lyn Valley still collapse due to scouring of the riverbank. Rebuilt sections of the stone wall skirting the road clearly show where this has taken place. A flood with the magnitude of August 1952 will inevitably change a river's course permanently in parts, as happened on this occasion. River response to rainfall since

*The original narrow channel of the West Lyn.*

the flood has been noticeably quicker due to extreme scouring of channels on the moor giving easier access to the flow of water. Any previous obstructions such as foliage and rocks that impeded flow were swept away. The course of streams became more direct which was clearly shown while temporary repairs were being carried out one September day soon after the flood. In Lynmouth, the West Lyn rose by 9 feet in 15 minutes shortly after heavy rainfall.

Some previously impassable bogs on the high moor became firm enough to walk on. Drainage of these areas had suddenly become more efficient caused by the excessive scouring of stormwater at the time.

Lyn rivers are prone to flooding no more than others in Britain, since 1953 when the channels were made wider and deeper, the village has only been threatened once. Extreme rainfall in 1958 brought the river level to the top of its banks, but that was the limit of the threat to the village. Flooding on only four occasions since 1952 has damaged footpaths from Watersmeet to Lynmouth along the East Lyn.

If heavy snow has fallen on Exmoor then the potential for flooding is at its greatest. Generally a fall of snow is consistent all over the high ground of the moor, and a thaw can bring a threatening amount of water thundering equally down both rivers. After heavy snow in the winter of 1982 had melted and combined with a rainfall of 3 inches, houses in Brendon were flooded. Since 1952, these houses have flooded four times, but it must be realised that the river channel here was not altered as in Lynmouth. Although no structural damage was caused to properties on these occasions, there was some movement of boulders in the East Lyn.

Responsibility of the Lyn rivers today is in the hands of the Environmental Agency that has now installed two level gauges. One is sited on the East Lyn at Brendon; the other is at Barbrook on the West Lyn. Three official rain gauges are situated at Brendon, Wistlandpound reservoir, Southwest of Lynmouth, and Blackpits Gate near Simonsbath. All these instruments would automatically telephone the Agency's head office in Exeter with information of threatening river levels or extreme rainfall, giving ample time to issue a warning to any areas threatened.

Depending on rainfall, the Lyn rivers spate to the point of flooding an average of once or twice a year and occasionally, movement of boulders can be detected. During a strong spate, boulders up to a ton can dislodge or move a short distance. Severe spates will have the same effect on 10 ton rocks. These movements are put into perspective when it is realised that some boulders of 40 and 50 tons were carried distances of at least a quarter of a mile during the 1952 flood. Boulders seen in the bed of both rivers are the result of landslides from the valley sides. If the reader is ever walking in the area and wishes to estimate the weight of a boulder, there is a simple formula to help.

Density of sandstone is 2.5 tons per cubic metre.
Weight = density x volume.
Therefore a boulder measuring, 2m x 2m x 2m has a volume of 8 cu metre.
Weight = 2.5 x 8. Boulder weighs 20 tons.

How peoples activities affected the flood is a question that occasionally comes to mind. On the high area of Exmoor where the Lyn rivers start there is no forestation, although the area has the name of Exmoor Forest. This title pertains to the time when Exmoor was a Royal hunting ground belonging to the Crown, although the Forest was rarely, if ever, used by Royalty due to its distance from the Court. Hypothetically, if the high ground of Exmoor had been an area of forestation, the amount of rainfall initially finding its way to the Lyn rivers would have been less. Consideration was given to forestation of some Exmoor areas after the flood but it was decided the advantages were not significant. Once trees and foliage had become saturated the water flow would increase, although run-off would still have been impeded to a degree. Large areas of woodland and foliage can absorb up to 3 inches of rain when in a dry state, but an area of high rainfall like Exmoor would give very little advantage at a time of extreme downpour.

As the village grew to meet demands from the early 19th century, necessitating building on the delta of the Lyn, then people did compound the tragic happening. In their mitigation the steep valley sides meant there was nowhere else to build, nobody could attach blame to a community that was responding to an opportunity that would ensure the survival of their village. A population that was dependent on a dwindling fishing trade, Lynmouth faced ruin, the villagers had no alternative.

There was no understanding of how frequently the village would suffer a flood of great magnitude, although one had happened in 1769, history did not repeat itself until 183 years later. The earlier flood may well have been as ferocious as 1952, however the 20th century village cannot be compared with how it was in the 18th century. Instead of being restricted by walls, the river was contained by natural sloping banks allowing it to disperse over a wider area reducing its velocity. Buildings were fewer and the bridge over the East Lyn was double-arched in those days.

It may happen again one day in Lynmouth, perhaps next year, perhaps in 200 years time. Of one thing we can be certain; the changes to the village will ensure it will cope better than any community in the country, if ever it is put to the test.

## Lynmouth Re-opens

*A month later, the village reopens...*

With regard to what the effects of the flood had on people and the area, the answer is - devastating. Before 1952, Lynmouth had a population of just over 450 permanent residents (this number could easily increase during the holiday season to 1700 people), today, there is just over 100 people. Over 200 buildings were in the village; 55 properties were either swept away, damaged beyond repair, or were demolished due to river widening and because of vulnerability if ever a flood of similar magnitude happened again. In addition, 72 properties had been damaged to a varying degree. Only two buildings erected in the village since 1952 have been built for habitation.

With this number of homes and businesses gone it was inevitable that the residential population would decrease significantly. Some left the village never to return while others moved to Lynton and eventually re-established their lives in the area. Most of those with homes still

*...trading again, a marked wall shows the flood level in Lynmouth Street.*

standing returned to the village when it re-opened a month after the flood and endeavoured to start again, but the village could never be the same.

Ironically the following few years brought more visitors to the resort than ever before due to the vast publicity it had received and the natural curiosity of people to a disaster. However, this increase of revenue to the village had been paid for with a price that was far too high.

The 1953 issue of the Lynton & Lynmouth guidebook published by the council every year contained a personal message from the chairman of Lynton Council. It read;

*"On behalf of the inhabitants of Lynton and Lynmouth, I wish to thank the people of Great Britain, the Empire and the world for their generous contributions which have put us on the road to recovery, so that we are now in a position to welcome old and new friends during the 1953 season.*

*The main features of the district are still unimpaired and the usual amenities are fully available, there being ample accommodation for everyone.*

*I do hope, therefore, that you will give us the opportunity of proving that a holiday may still be enjoyed in the Lynton and Lynmouth district as in previous years.*

*Signed Dorothy Slater".*

*Lynmouth returns - never to be the same.*

Sadly that year there were more advertisements for hotels in Lynton than for Lynmouth. Some well-known and popular establishments such as the Lyndale, Lyn Valley, Falls, Granville and Beach Hotels were never to advertise again.

There is one question that is often asked when thinking especially of the thirty-four people who lost their lives in the disaster. Could the flood have been predicted? The answer is no, certainly not as far as the extremity of the flood is concerned. During the day of 15th August, river levels had risen bringing an air of excitement to people in the village. In the early evening when the river was near the top of its banks there was concern shown by visitors who were not used to the river levels, but no sign of panic. Locals were not unduly worried, even when the banks started to overflow; they had seen it had happen in the past. Nobody could have envisaged or even dreamt of what was to follow later that evening.

There were no level gauges sited on the riverbanks that would give an official warning to those in the village. Besides, in those days the reading of river gauges were taken by eye and access to them that night would have been impossible. It was the extreme rainfall of over 5.9 inches between 7.30 and 11.30pm that when reaching the village later compounded the flooding. There was no warning, the amount of rain that fell, the character of the Lyn rivers, the blocking of bridges causing surges in flow and exaggerated levels of water all combined to create a happening that nobody could have foreseen or been prepared for.

*Shelley's Cottage Hotel, later rebuilt.*

## Facts & Figures

The fund financed the Flood Memorial Hall which now houses an exhibition of photographs and a model of old Lynmouth. The Hall replaced the Village Institute that had been a room above the lifeboat house washed away by the flood. Not only commemorating the disaster, the Hall's opening on 10th July 1958 officially marked the completion of the rebuilding of Lynmouth which in total had cost £707,191 (1957 value). It had been 5 years and 11 months since that fateful night.

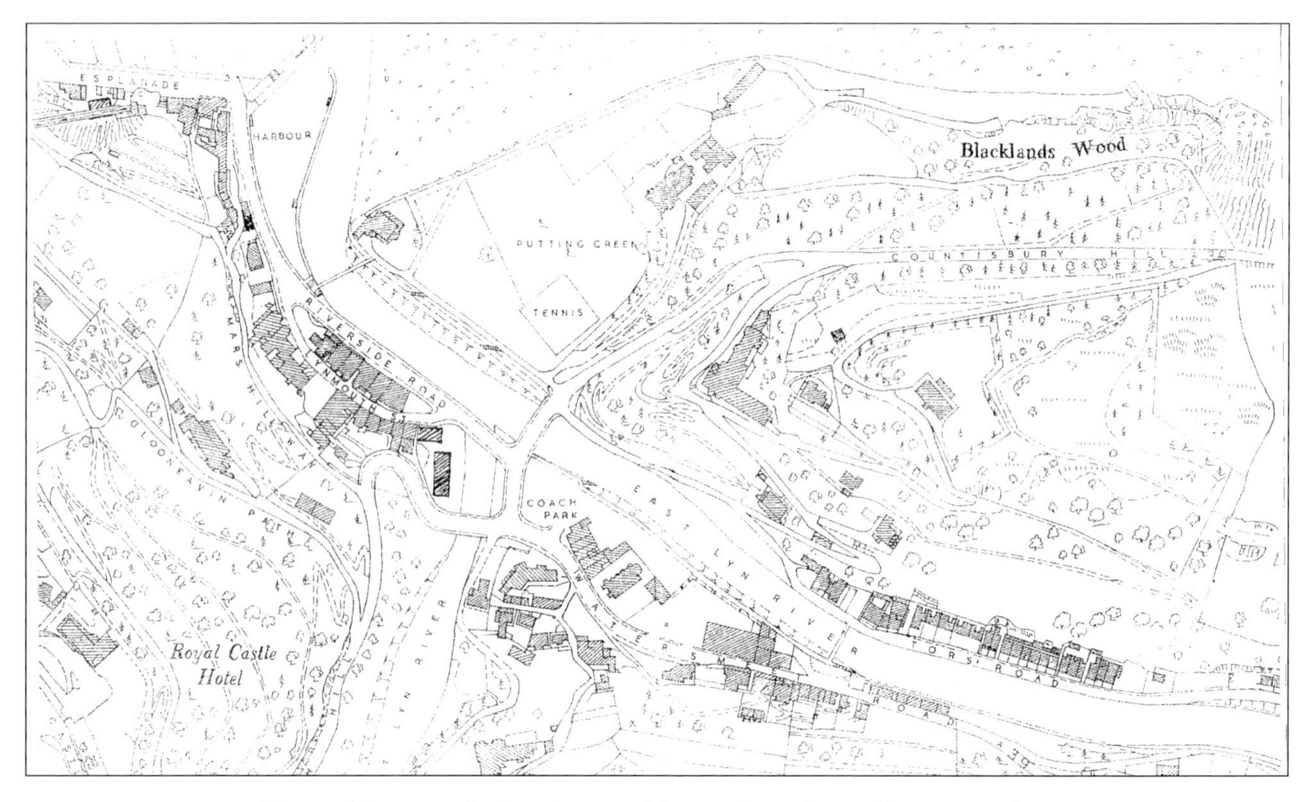


*Plan of Lynmouth showing positions of roads and houses today.*

According to Bleasdale and Douglas (1952), 90,000,000 tons of rain fell on North Devon and West Somerset that day and 14,260,000 tons of water flowed through Lynmouth village in 24 hours. Although money donated to the Flood Fund was distributed to the 1,710 people who had suffered losses, an amount was used to finance some private and community projects. The cost of work carried out on various private roads, bridges, and river walls for instance was reimbursed by a fund payment of £26,993.

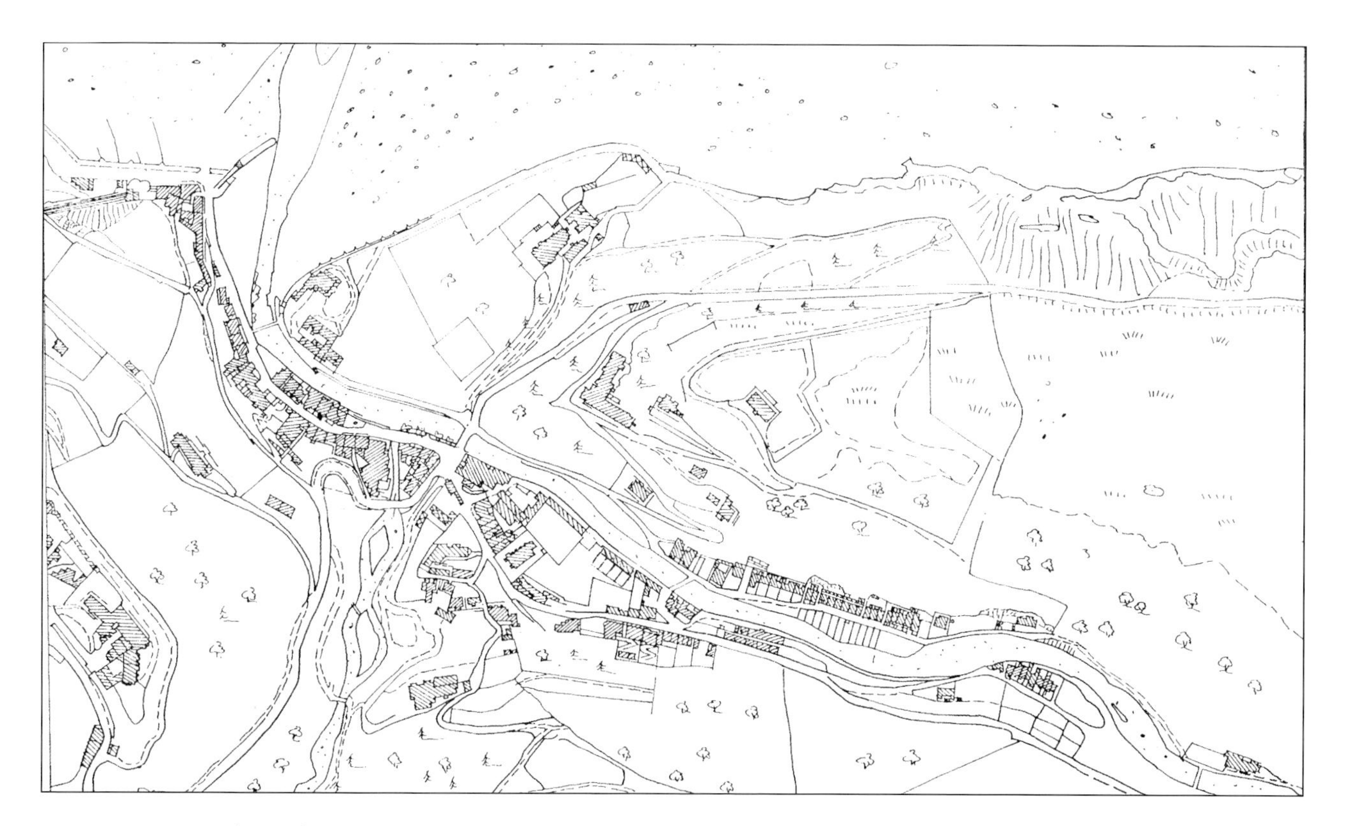

*Plan of Lynmouth showing positions of roads and houses before the flood.*

| Deaths: | 17 at Lynmouth |
|---|---|
| | 11 at Barbrook near Lynmouth |
| | 3 at Filliegh nr South Molton |
| | 3 at Parracombe nr Lynton |
| Total | 34 |

From a total of 212 properties in Lynmouth;

31 swept away

34 partly demolished - 12 beyond repair

26 damaged

12 lost to river-widening

A total of 55 buildings were lost in Lynmouth - approximately 25% of the rateable properties in the village.

From a total of 46 properties at Barbrook;

5 swept away

12 damaged

A total of 5 properties were lost.

| | |
|---|---|
| Buildings lost or damaged beyond repair in other areas | 43 |
| Roads & lanes damaged | 110 |
| Bridges destroyed or damaged beyond repair. | 28 |
| Motor vehicles lost, or damaged beyond repair | 95 |
| Motor cycles | 10 |
| Caravans | 4 |
| Motor coaches | 1 |
| Lorries | 2 |
| Debris removed from village / Lyn Rivers | 114,000 Tons |
| Flood fund (when closed in August 1956) | £1,336,425 |

## Cloud Seeding

The great storm that created the 1952 flood had originated with a small depression in the northeast Atlantic. During the Exmoor storm, violent up-draughts of warm moisture-laden air near its centre gave rise to the torrential rain. Some visitors who were up on the high ground of Exmoor told of seeing the unusual sight of pink lightening shortly before the storm broke.

It is sometimes alleged that secret government experiments with the weather may have contributed to the reasons that caused the Lynmouth flood. It is also thought by some that perhaps the extreme amount of rain that fell over Exmoor in 1952 was unnatural. Unusual it certainly was, but that amount of rain had been experienced in Britain twice in the previous thirty-five years before the Lynmouth flood, and could not be classed as unnatural. In 1946 the Ministry of Defence in conjunction with the RAF first carried out secret experiments with cloud seeding. Various substances were dropped into clouds by aeroplane to precipitate rainfall. Theoretically it was claimed that solid carbon dioxide (dry ice) or silver iodide, would be the most effective ingredients to use. If introduced into subfreezing levels of a liquid cloud, the dry ice would directly freeze the liquid water, precipitating rainfall. Silver iodide, which has a crystal lattice structure similar to ice, would create artificial ice nuclei when dropped into a liquid cloud creating a similar effect. However, theory does not always prove itself when applied practically and experiments stopped in 1955.

Due to the resulting failures to successfully create rainfall, cloud seeding experiments throughout hot and arid areas of the world have virtually disappeared since 1985.

Suspicions of local inhabitants were never aroused or attention drawn to any aeroplanes flying over Exmoor on days or nights leading up to the time of the flood.

An experiment to precipitate rain was carried out over Bedfordshire on 14th August, the day before the flood. As that area is 160 miles north-east of Exmoor and the weather was and had been travelling in an easterly direction, the material facts appear to contradict any suspicious theories put forward.

Attempts to modify extreme weather conditions to our advantage throughout the world have been and still are very occasionally carried out. For instance, weakening hurricanes, suppressing fog, diminishing hailstones or any threatening meteorological conditions.

A fall of 3 inches of rain in one day is regarded as exceptional, and yet since 1865 when records began, figures exceeding that amount in Britain have caused major floods with considerable loss of life and damage involved. It is a fact that exceptional rainfall in Britain is more common than is realised and has been since before records were kept.

## Future

An increasing population requiring more areas of available land has resulted in building on potential flood sites throughout Britain and indeed throughout the world. Not only on comparatively flat areas where water has room to spread and disperse, but also in valleys where floodwater is constricted causing higher levels and greater velocities causing increased damage. When planning these developments, consideration should be given not only to recent river flooding, but also to extreme events in the area over a long period.

The Lynmouth Flood of 15th August 1952 was tragically the worst river flood disaster in British history. If buildings continue to be erected on the flood plains of Britain's rivers without adequate protection, there is no reason why this unique North Devon village should not lose that unenviable title one-day in the future.

*Lynmouth today.*

One quarter of the buildings in Lynmouth were never replaced. Since the immediate loss of population there has been a continued gradual decline of permenant residents, followed by the subsequent loss of service shops and ultimately the community's independence.

Today, Lynmouth relies entirely on tourism and caters efficiently for its many visitors.

The rivers no longer pose a threat but the village has lost much of its intimacy. Sadly the nooks and crannys that gave a rambling appearance achieved over centuries of erratic additions have largely gone.

However, the essence of Lynmouth remains, for that is within its locale. It will forever be "England's Little Switzerland".

*Lynmouth harbour circa 1900. Turbal Rock can be seen encroaching into the harbour from the road on the left. This rock protected the cottages on Mars Hill from the flood.*

*Today, the harbour is of a similar size but the road has been widened covering Turbal Rock. The cottages on Mars Hill remain.*

*Backs of Lynmouth Street buildings circa 1940*

*The same view today, Riverside Road has been built where the river was. Seen here with the tide in demonstrates how close to the water the ground floor of these buildings would have been.*

## Glossary

| | |
|---|---|
| Cusec | Cubic feet of water per second. |
| Design flow | Size of channel carrying normal volume of water. |
| Downcutting | Erosion of valley by river flow. |
| Peak flow | Size of channel carrying maximum volume of water. |
| Surge | Sudden increase in volume and amount of water. |

Further reading on subjects covered in this book can be found in the following publications;


| | |
|---|---|
| The Lynmouth Flood Disaster | Eric Delderfield. |
| The Lynmouth Flood Disaster - A village guide | Tim Prosser |
| Lyn in Flood. | Peter Keene / Derek Elsom.Thematic Trails, Oxford Brookes University, Oxford. |
| Valley of Rocks Lynton. | Peter Keene / Brian Pearce.Thematic Trails, Oxford Brookes University, Oxford |
| Lynmouth Lifeboat | John Loveless. Lyndale Photographic Publications, Lynmouth. |


## Acknowledgments

My sincere thanks go to dear friends who painfully recalled to me their memories of that terrible night in 1952. I am especially grateful to John Loveless for his patient guidance during the publication of this book. Thanks must be given to the people of Lynton and Lynmouth for encouraging me to write a story that is still emotive to villagers. To my family, I thank them for their patience. To Gordon Potter, a thank you for tuition on the mysterious workings of a word processor. I offer extreme thanks to my mother Peggy who has always given her generous support to any project I have undertaken. This book would not have been written without the understanding and encouragement of my wife; to Marcia, a sincere thank you.

My thanks and appreciation is given to the following people and organisations.
Janet Atkins, Barnstaple Records Office, Helen Chalk, Jack Chubb, Devon & Cornwall Constabulary, Dorothy Dimmock, Environmental Agency Exeter, Fred & Freda Fouracre, Wally Gilson, Derek R.A. Harper GM, Bill Harris, Des Hobbs, Andrew Litson, Guy Litson, Lynton & Lynmouth Town Council, Betty Massie (Dulverton Heritage Centre), Meteorological Office Bracknell, Phlip Nichols, Edward Nightingale, Ken Oxenham, John Pedder, Jean Pile (nee Bale), Joan Powell (nee Taylor), Roy Pugsley, Valerie Robson (nee Bevan), John Travis.
Grateful thanks are given to the following people and organisations for their permission to reproduce illustrations and graphics in this book.

| | |
|---|---|
| Janet Atkins: | page 6. |
| Daily Express: | pages 41, 42, 44. |
| Devon and Cornwall Constabulary: | pages 11(bottom), 18(right), 19, 22(right), 25, 30, 31. 32(top), 33, 35(bottom), 39, 48, 49(bottom). |
| Dulverton Heritage Centre: | page 58. |
| Bill Durman | page 29(right) with kind permission of Terry Richards. |
| Fred Fouracre: | page 16. |
| Derek Harper GM: | page 43. |
| Peter Keene: | page 4. |
| Knights of Barnstaple: | page 60. |
| Terry Loveless: | pages 90, 91. |
| Lyndale Photographic: | pages 2, 3(left), 5, 8, 9, 10, 11(top), 12, 13, 17, 18(left), 20, 22(left), 23, 24, 26, 28, 35(top), 38, 40, 56, 70, 77, 80, 81,84, 94, 95, 97(bottom), 96, back cover, front cover; (top & bottom). |
| Meteorlogical Office, Bracknell: | pages 67, 68. |
| Tim Prosser: | pages 3 (right),29 left 31(bottom), 51, 73, 74, 75, 76, 95(top), front cover (centre). |
| Bill Pryor: | pages 14, 45, 46, 47, 49(top), 50, 52, 53, 54, 69. |
| Rev. Philip Ringer: | page 63. |
| Sunday Pictorial: | pages 87, 88, 89. |

The model of old Lynmouth pictured on page 70 was made by Tim Prosser.

## About the author

As a 10-year-old living in Wales, the dramatic newspaper photographs of the Lynmouth flood left a deep impression on Tim Prosser. After a career in engineering he moved to Lynton in 1996 and, with the patient understanding of his wife Marcia, constructed a scale model of pre-flood Lynmouth in their dining room. While researching for the model, local flood survivors gave him a personal insight of the disaster. Listening to these emotive stories encouraged Tim to write *The Lynmouth Flood Disaster.*

The model can be viewed in the Lynmouth Flood Memorial Hall from Easter until October, and at St John The Baptist church, Lynmouth during the winter months.